"The Noise
of Threatening Drum"

"The Noise
of Threatening Drum"

Dramatic Strategy and Political Ideology
in Shakespeare and the English Chronicle Plays

Larry S. Champion

DELAWARE

Newark: University of Delaware Press
London and Toronto: Associated University Presses

Associated University Presses
440 Forsgate Drive
Cranbury, NJ 08512

Associated University Presses
25 Sicilian Avenue
London WC1A 2QH, England

Associated University Presses
P.O. Box 488, Port Credit
Mississauga, Ontario
Canada L5G 4M2

The paper used in this publication meets the requirements
of the American National Standard for Permanence of Paper
for Printed Library Materials Z39.48-1984.

Library of Congress Cataloging-in-Publication Data

Champion, Larry S.
    The noise of threatening drum : dramatic strategy and political
ideology in Shakespeare and the English chronicle plays / Larry S. Champion.
        p.   cm.
    Includes bibliographical references.
    ISBN 0-87413-387-4 (alk. paper)
    1. Shakespeare, William 1564–1616—Histories.   2. Shakespeare,
William, 1564–1616—Political and social views.   3. English drama—
Early modern and Elizabethan, 1500–1600—History and criticism.
4. Historical drama, English—History and criticism.   5. Politics in
literature.   I. Title.
PR2982.C47   1990
822.3'3—dc20   89-40380
                                                                                     CIP

PRINTED IN THE UNITED STATES OF AMERICA

Contents

Acknowledgments

Anyone who works in the field of English Renaissance drama is profoundly dependent upon the efforts of many others, and I have attempted to recognize the most important of these debts in the documentation. My own research has also been facilitated through partial release from teaching duties, and for this I thank John Bassett and the Department of English at North Carolina State University. Moreover, I am happy to acknowledge the suggestions of particular individuals who have read portions or all of the manuscript—Deborah T. Curren-Aquino, C. R. Forker, Richard Helgerson, Barbara Mowat, Paul Werstine, and Heather Dubrow. I am grateful, also, to Charlene Turner and Carol Sharpe for preparation of the manuscript and to Lauren Lepow and Cynthia Crumrine for careful editorial work. My greatest debt, as usual, is to my wife, Nancy.

Portions of this study, in somewhat different form, have appeared previously as "'Answer to This Perilous Time': Political Ideology in *The Reign of King Edward III*," *English Studies* 69 (1988): 117–29; "'By Conquest Mine, By Usurpation Thine': Perspective and Politics in *Edmund Ironside*," *Studies in Philology* 85 (1988): 211–24; "The 'Un-End' of *King John:* Shakespeare's Demystification of Closure," in *"King John": New Perspectives*, ed. Deborah T. Curren-Aquino (Newark: University of Delaware Press, 1989), 173–85; "'What Prerogative Means': Perspective and Political Ideology in *The Famous Victories of Henry V*," *South Atlantic Review* 53, No. 4 (1988): 1–19; and 'Dramatic Strategy and Political Ideology in *The Life and Death of Thomas, Lord Cromwell*," *Studies in English Literature* 29 (1989): 219–36. I appreciate permission to reprint these materials as a portion of this larger study.

Introduction

This collection brings together discussions of political ideology in thirteen representative English Renaissance history plays, both Shakespearean and non-Shakespearean. Included are the anonymous *The Famous Victories of Henry V* and *Edward III*, the apocryphal plays *Sir John Oldcastle* and *Thomas, Lord Cromwell*, the pseudo-Shakespearean *Edmund Ironside*, and Shakespeare's *1, 2, 3 Henry VI, King John, Richard II, 1, 2 Henry IV*, and *Henry V*. London in the late sixteenth century witnessed a remarkable outburst of such drama fictionalizing history by framing stories from the lives of well-known English statesmen and monarchs of past years. In the twenty-year period from 1586 to 1606, the *Annals of English Drama*—excluding categories like "classical," "biblical," "foreign," and "allegorical"—records eighty-four history plays.[1] Their popularity peaked in the final years of Elizabeth's reign, with thirty-one appearing in 1597–98. It is traditional to attribute this hybrid dramatic form to a tide of patriotism cresting in the struggle against Catholic Spain; these plays, according to Schelling, seek "to inspire in [their] auditors the impulses of pride in country and patriotism."[2] Coleridge envisioned the action as arousing "a love of just liberty, and a respect for all those fundamental institutions of social life, which bind men together."[3] Dealing with the fate of a nation,[4] they furnish "examples of the political course of the world, applicable to all times";[5] they provide a political mirror[6] concerning the science of government and the fine art of politics.[7] In the years around the defeat of the Armada that mark this great popularity, these plays, like the medieval chronicles earlier, serve as a memorial to great national heroes.[8]

The essential difficulty with such an approach is that it assumes both an audience basically sympathetic to the monarchy and a universal perspective in plays that, in fact, are designed to appeal to, and to engage the emotional interests of, as many spectators as possible. The exact nature of the Elizabethan popular audience is a matter of sharp critical debate. Alfred Harbage has argued that it was some 94 percent dealers, craftsmen, laborers, and servants—primarily a "working-class audience [reflecting] the

9

great numerical superiority of working classes in London";[9] and Robert Weimann's study, more recently, has claimed that the Elizabethan theaters "were still dependent on large plebeian audiences."[10] Ann Jennalie Cook, on the other hand, has asserted just the opposite, that London's socially free or privileged set "ruled the playgoing world quite as frankly as they ruled the political world, the mercantile world, and the rest of the cultural world."[11] If Harbage assumed too readily, perhaps, that what we would now call the lower-middle and lower classes had the time and the financial resources to attend the theater with regularity, Cook appears to be equally extreme in virtually excluding these spectators altogether. Stephen Booth notes, for example, how misleading her demographic and economic statistics could be in determining the clientele of movies or of afternoon baseball games played on working days in America in the 1930s.[12] And Martin Butler observes that official directives aimed at controlling the statutory working hours of artificers "cut two ways, revealing the existence of practices to be legislated against;[13] further, he demonstrates how easily one can dispute Cook's conclusions by marshaling evidence to support the assumption that laborers, craftsmen, and apprentices did attend the theaters in large numbers. For Andrew Gurr, most recently, it is the sliding-price scale of admission that compellingly argues for a distribution of social classes in the playhouses.[14] Certainly, from the diverse comments of such men as William Harrison, John Stowe, Henry Crosse, Stephen Gosson, Philip Stubbes, Thomas Coryat, Thomas Heywood, Thomas Dekker, Ben Jonson, Thomas Wilson, and George Wither, and from such documents as the *Calendar of State Papers*, the *Acts of the Privy Council*, and *Documents Relating to the Office of the Master of the Revels*, there is no scarcity of conflicting information. In any case, the evidence suggests that, whatever the precise ratio between privileged and nonprivileged and whatever the fluctuation of such a ratio from one year to another, there must indeed have been a socially mixed theater audience.

That the audience was primarily plebeian, working-class, or privileged would not, of course, rigidly dictate the response of any particular individual; nor would such a mixed gathering necessarily have been disruptive by nature. Nevertheless, if the response had indeed been monolithic, preachers like Thomas White would not have described the theaters as "a continuall monument of London's prodigalitie and Folly."[15] Nor would the authorities have been continually alarmed about these public gatherings as "centres of potential social unrest and as dens of iniquity which

made people restive,"[16] "as a troublesome and pote*
sive social phenomenon that threatened religious an
chies and yet, despite considerable antagonism, cou
outlawed nor put down."[17] "Power," as Michel Fou
"was what was seen, what was shown, and what was
and, parodoxically, found the principle of its force i
ments by which it deployed that force."[18] While the power of the
stage provided an avenue of social and cultural control, it also
produced "an expanded self-awareness that the period in question was not fully equipped to manage or turn to its advantage."[19]
Admittedly, for the aristocracy and the London authorities, the
surface political ideology of chronicle play after chronicle play
seems to provide a "rationalization of [the] class's social position
and material interests;"[20] but, as D. M. Palliser observes, such a
cult of monarchism "reflects a position in need of buttressing
rather than one of unassailable strength."[21]

It is difficult, at best, to envision all segments of the audience
responding in patriotic exaltation to plays that simplistically
marginalized genuine social problems even while focusing on political ideas "deeply rooted in the emotions of the age."[22] England
in the last decades of the century was suffering from famine, discontent, faction, and social dislocation. Enclosures for sheep graz-
ing "had uprooted tens of thousands and emptied whole villages
yet had provided no work for the dispossessed."[23] Inflation was
rampant, as prices rose 79 percent between 1559 and 1602, while
wages in most counties remained almost unchanged from 1580
to 1640.[24] One demonstrable effort to keep a pool of cheap labor
available to support the aristocratic system was the Statute of
Artificers, passed in 1563, which stipulated that children should
not be allowed to depart from the occupation of the parent; and
as late as 1610 "any able-bodied man or woman who should
threaten to run away from his or her parish was liable to be sent
to the house of correction and treated as a vagabond."[25] Certainly
one might question Christopher Hill's assumptions that such a law
would benefit the aristocratic system more than the mercantile
system, just as one might question Lawrence Stone's sweeping assertions concerning the development of "affective individualism"
and the subsequent "decline of loyalties to lineage, kin, patron
and local community" and the corresponding rise of a family
"organized around the principle of personal autonomy."[26] Even
so, the conclusion is unmistakable that respect for the aristocracy
and for their authority was diminished and that the English society was sorely troubled and divided. Inevitably, "as society came

gradually to be seen, not as a divinely sanctioned institution, but as an aggregate of individuals united by no more lofty principle than self-interest, kinship lost its special sanctity."[27] Given such volatile conditions in what Terry Eagleton has recently described as a "class society in crisis,"[28] the government, understandably, was "obsessed with the fear of revolts, riots, and armed assaults"[29] as the rampant individualism of both the old aristocracy and the most aggressive section of the bourgeoisie began to offer a real challenge to the power of the monarchy.

If analyses focusing on the interaction of drama with the forces of social conflict are still relatively rare, one must remember that criticism begets criticism. As Malcolm Evans has recently noted, the text is never simply itself, but what it has become; "the encrustation of all previous criticism has been shaped and altered by past thought," and the evolution may be deadly in terms of the author's original intentions or apprehensions.[30] The "reconciliatory strategy of conventional literary scholarship has been committed to a view of literature as a benign, and thus culturally and politically innocuous, institution."[31] Thus, for the most part, readings of the chronicle plays have worked within variations of the assumption that the plays affirm and support—or, at the very least, do not defy—the Tudor establishment. A half century ago, for instance, even a critic who presumed to question whether it should be the function of literature to espouse "the glorification of war and the adulation of sovereigns" was satisfied to focus his attention on "how the love of England expressed itself in the English drama of Elizabeth's reign."[32]

Within the past two decades or so critics have steadily chipped away at the assumption that the history plays were written as little more than dramatic panegyrics.[33] Interest instead has begun to focus on the playwright's depiction of a monarch in such a way that his motivations and actions are subject to multiple interpretations. Moreover, secondary characters and diversionary episodes can point to flaws either in the ruler or in the society, often exposing the seam between the rhetoric of patriotism and national harmony, on the one hand, and the reality of social conditions and the Machiavellian schemes by which power is maintained, on the other. Usually such plays provoke one of two divergent responses, depending upon the political and social orientation that the individual spectator brings to the playhouse. Superficially, the actions appear to support the general aristocratic assumptions of class, privilege, and, in some cases, monarchical absolutism; other scenes, however, seem to counterpoint this view, either interrogating those assumptions of power or reflecting the suffering and political dislocation of the nonprivileged.

The focus of discussion in each of the following chapters is on how the chronicle plays are framed to permit—indeed to encourage—a multiplicity of ideological responses; responses that, in turn, accommodate and stimulate the divergent political views of a socially heterogenuous audience. If, for instance, the essay on *Edmund Ironside* was prompted by Eric Sams' recent claim for Shakespearean authorship, the primary concern is more with the structure and political implications of the play. In many ways wooden in characterization and highly rhetorical in style, it nonetheless bears a strong antimonarchic tone. Moreover, the scheming villain who delights in his own wit and the success of his machinations and who, through soliloquies and asides, shares a private level of perception with the spectators, invites comparison with Marlowe's Barabas and Shakespeare's Richard III; similarly, though Canutus and Edmund are psychologically more simplistic, the conflict of mighty opposites is not unlike the juxtaposition of Mortimer and Edward II or Bullingbrook and Richard II. The question of when *Edmund Ironside* was written ultimately emerges as a more compelling issue than who wrote it.

In any attempt to come to terms with the manner in which English playwrights in the 1590s (and Shakespeare in particular) depict English history, *King John* stands as a pivotal work. The focus here is on how historical process is transformed into human process, stripped bare of Tudor providentialism and reduced to an individual self-interest that only in its best moments might be communally enlightened. Denied the reassurance of traditional closure, the spectator confronts in John a starkly ambiguous character who is simultaneously a usurper, a would-be murderer, a terror-stricken capitulator, a sufferer, a patriot, and a kingly defender of his nation against the avarice of France and the superstition of Rome. The future Henry plays bear witness to the complexity of this concept of history—with martial valor counterpointed by the pragmatics of survival in one, political efficiency counterpointed by a gradual but inevitable process of dehumanization in another, and the heroics of national ambition counterpointed by occasional glimpses of the price of that dehumanization and the grim reminder of the brevity of both life and empire in yet another.

While the individual works covered in this study are admittedly only representative of a wide range of chronicle plays, they share a remarkably consistent concern both for the means by which stage presentations were intended to interact with their particular audiences and for the qualities of innovation and experimentation by which the social boundaries of drama were broadened and expanded. In effect, they provide a variety of viewpoints through which to capture what Julia Briggs has called the "age's increasingly conflicting values and standards [set forth] in terms of urgently opposed individual convictions."[34] Operating at the level of the political agenda that the particular individual brings to the playhouse, they force the spectators—beyond the pleasures or the anxieties of the moment—into a kind of vicarious involvement in the complexities and ambiguities that comprise society and the often devious means by which government establishes and maintains itself.

"The Noise
of Threatening Drum"

1

The Famous Victories of Henry V

Dated anywhere from 1574 to 1588,[1] *The Famous Victories of Henry V* is generally considered significant only as what is perhaps the earliest extant example of the English history play or as the raw substance from which Shakespeare fashioned much of the material in his trilogy on the reigns of Henry IV and Henry V. If the occasional critic concedes a "power of expresion and a sense of human realities"[2] or notes its importance in the development of pre-Shakespearean drama,[3] it is more often condemned as "formless and incoherent,"[4] as a trivial and episodic "stringing together of events in mere temporal succession,"[5] or as "a play of incredible meanness."[6] Such criticism, while reflecting the relatively primitive qualities of plot and character by comparison with the history plays yet to come, especially those of Shakespeare, fails to address the fact that the early audiences apparently responded quite enthusiastically to the political issues central to the play. Whatever, its relative demerits, *The Famous Victories* enjoyed a considerable popularity, becoming one of the "great standbys of the professional troupes in the years before Henslowe began his diary."[7] Performed by the "Queenes Maiesties Players" at the Bull Inn sometime before Richard Tarlton's death in 1588, the play was entered in the *Stationers' Register* in 1594 and first published in a quarto of 1598.[8] Claims for authorship have included Tarleton,[9] Samuel Rowley,[10] the earl of Oxford,[11] and the young Shakespeare.[12]

The traditional view of the play is that its "chief shaping attitude is patriotism,"[13] its basis, the "growing national spirit."[14] A "heroic folk play with an historical figure as its hero,"[15] it represents "spectacular patriotism"[16] in the tradition that "war must be glorious if it is to stir men's enthusiasm."[17] Through such an experience, we are to suppose, those in the audience corporately sense a "strong current of national feeling," a kind of "embodiment of England's glory"[18] as they witness, in Tillyard's words, "a providential view of history in terms of the official Tudor interpretation of earlier events."[19]

For a spectator inclined to view the action from another perspective, however, the political ideology is radically different. The piont is not that *The Famous Victories of Henry V,* or any other drama of the period, mirrors the contemporary social background in any precise or exact manner, but that the spectator's response to the political issues of a particular chronicle play inevitably would be affected to some extent by his own social status and his attitude toward monarchic authority. In any event, a glance beyond the monarchophilia and patriotic glitter reveals a sordid world of political treachery, a play in which putative honor bows to greed and kingly solicitude is transformed into political exploitation, an aristocratic world of crass legal manipulation, a prince/king satiated with a sense of power to the point of utter disregard for the public welfare, a world foregrounding the horrors and brutalities of a war with, as its special prey, commoners unwittingly victimized by confrontations within the power structure of their society. The dramatic strategy is not essentially unlike that of Shakespeare's later *Henry V,* which "deftly registers every nuance of royal hypocrisy, ruthlessness, and bad faith, but does so in the context of a celebration, a collective panegyric to 'this star of England,' the charismatic leader who purges the commonwealth of its incorrigibles and forges the martial national state."[20]

From such a perspective, more specifically, Hal's actions as heir apparent both denigrate the monarchy and reflect the plight of the commoners in such a society. His crass disregard for the traditional ritualistic values of the crown emphasizes his concern only for personal pleasure and for the material benefits that accrue from a privileged position above the law. The result, for the spectators inclined to this view, is a demystification of the royal house and an exposure of the corruption at its center. Twice Hal remarks to his companions in crime that, if "the king my father were dead, we would all be kings" (127–8, 628–9),[21] noting elsewhere that "the breath shal be no sooner out of his [father's] mouth but I will clap the crowne on my head. . . . I stand vpon thorns til the crowne be on my head" (662–64, 672–74). Having robbed his father's agents, he gloats over the booty and swears to spend fully half of it in debauchery before the night has passed.

Even more revealing is his disdain for those of lower social standing, whether in his peremptory insistence that his companions must celebrate with him in a tavern in Eastcheap even though they all prefer an inn in Feversham, or in his terrorizing the poor fellows whom he has robbed. The latter, who fear they will be hanged if they return to court without the king's money, are no less intimidated by the prince himself. They full well know that those who robbed them rode Hal's "blacke nag" and Oldcastle's "bay hobbie" and that one was "about the bignesse of [Hal]" (92), but they dare not accuse one of royal blood. He greets with abusive disdain their hesitation even to speak to the prince: "Sowns, vilains, speak, or Ile cut off your heads!" (70–71). When they identify themselves, he taunts them with the assumption that they have brought him money; and their reference to his horse provokes his snide response, "Blood, you vilains! my father robd of his money abroad, and we robd in our stables!" (86–88). Forced to sue for grace in the face of the prince's threats, they are sworn to silence about the robbery and mocked mercilessly the moment they are offstage: "was not this brauely done? For now the vilaines dare not speake a word of it, I haue so feared them with words" (108–10).

Although Hal is twice arrested for blatantly criminal activities, the anonymous playwright in both instances depicts the opprobrium of royal prerogative that utilizes the law to maintain order among the masses while manipulating it in a crassly self-serving manner. Within an hour of Hal's first imprisonment, for example, a messenger from the court arrives "in all haste" (281–82), with the consequence not only that the prince is immediately released but also that the sheriff and the lord mayor of London are summoned to appear before the king himself. If the king, in a manner cleverly designed for maximum public political benefit, ultimately praises his officers for upholding the law, he most assuredly has made his point for royal authority. Following his personal remonstrations that his son is "not to be halled to prison by euery subject" (318–19) and their timorous response that the prince while in prison "want[ed] nothing that [was] fit for his Grace and your Maiesties sonne," he heavy-handedly forces them to wait offstage while he deliberates their fate. Hal's subsequent imprisonment for boxing the lord chief justice's ear is no less brief, his release coming before Sir John Oldcastle can even get to the Fleet to visit him. Most noticeable in this scene is Hal's arrogance, both in his insistence that the thief, his "man" convicted of robbery, be freed and in his gloating over the law's inability to contain him:

> Didst thou not know that I am a princes son? Why, tis inough for me to looke into a prison, though I come not in my-selfe. . . . I tel you, sirs, when I am king we will haue no such things. (620–23, 626–27)

He promises to expel the lord chief justice (replacing him with his boon companion, Ned), to convert prisons into fencing schools, and to provide a commendation and an annual pension for highwaymen. He, moreover, directly mocks the idea that he is "a well toward yoong man" (689) merely sowing his wild oats who, in the fullness of time, will cast aside his idle habits.

Central to the traditional reading of Henry as ideal prince is his sudden repentance in the presence of his dying father, a character transformation Prior admits does not develop logically from the first half of the play[22] and Tillyard claims can only be termed a miracle.[23] Again, though, these scenes represent a strategy of containment, to a different perspective foregrounding a young man on the brink of grasping power who, consistent with the earlier Hal, is flagrantly manipulative and disdainful of both father and friend. He arrives at court with his companions (called by Oxford a "verie disordered company" [729]), rapping loudly on the palace gates and badgering a porter, who attempts to maintain civility. When the sick Henvy IV twice specifies that this "vilde and reprobate company" (751–52) is not to be admitted, Hal—infuriated with the rebuff just as he was earlier with that of the lord chief justice—dismisses the group, calls for "three noyse of musitians" (746), and enters his father's chamber "with a dagger in his hand." What happens next is crucial to the idea of a spiritually reborn Hal as, we are told, he comes upon his father weeping, speaks *in an aside* "My conscience accuseth me" (764), *kneels* by the king's bed, and laments his sinful ways and his unworthiness to inherit the crown. In fact, however, both the assumption that he speaks in an aside and that he kneels are editorial interpolations, not stage directions in the text. More plausibly, dagger in hand (as specifically stipulated by a stage direction), he approaches his father "ready," as Ribner notes, "to murder him for the crown,"[24] when, to his surprise, he finds the king conscious and suddenly blurts out directly to the intended victim his determination to reform. Such action not only covers his original scheme to take the king's life; the resulting reconciliation with his father also solidifies his expectations for the crown.

This assumption that his repentance has been more politically expedient than genuine makes all the more plausible the fact that, when we next see him, he speaks of having neglected for so long visiting his sick father (859) and that the king berates him anew: "I had thought that the last time I had you in schooling I had giuen you a lesson for all; and do you now begin againe?" (897–900). But once more, whether sincere or expedient, Hal's scheme works. He proclaims that his tears were genuine,[25] and his father proceeds to invest him with the crown on the spot: "let me put thee in possession whilst I liue, that no man may depriue thee of it after my death" (924–26). From his father's comment and his haste to secure the crown for his son, it must be inferred only that Henry fears forces in the court which would not wish the crown to be so descended. More pointedly, although both Oxford and Exeter mouth approval of Henry's action, incredibly claiming that Hal's "former life" betokens a successful reign (949), there apparently are others who are willing to look at the prince's former life-style more objectively and draw quite different conclusions. In any case, Hal's first words when in possession of the crown strike neither a note of moral contrition nor of concern for the stability of the country, but one of cold, steely power politics: "now I haue it from you, and from you I will keepe it. And he that seekes to take the crowne from my head, let him looke that his armour be thicker then mine" (937–41).

Changes that the anonymous author made in his source directly support this reading. According to Raphael Holinshed in his account published in 1577, the first confrontation between father and son is occasioned by Prince Henry's coming to court to clear his name of slanderous reports of his conduct spread by those who wish to sow discord within the very heart of the royal family. Appareled in "a gowne of blew satten, full of small oilet holes, at euerie hole the needle hanging by a silke thred with which it was sewed" (details used in the play), he brings with him a group of noblemen and "other his freends that wished him well."[26] Those in his company modestly refuse to advance farther than the fire, at which point the king, borne to a privy chamber, meets with Hal "in the presence of three or four persons" (54). The prince delcares his innocence of any evil intention and offers his father his dagger "in all humble reuerence," urging the king to dispatch his life forthwith if any suspicions remain. Clearly the playwright *adds* the rowdy company that the king twice bars from the room, *adds* both Hal's entering the room alone and his carrying a drawn dagger, and *omits* his offering the dagger to the king in a sacrificial posture. Each of these alterations is calculated to render the Hal of the play more devious and degenerate; to insist that he speak in an aside in order to indicate a sudden change of heart flies in the face of the very pattern the author has demonstrably labored to produce.

Prince Henry in Holinshed also lacks any Machiavellian touch in the second encounter with his father. Having set the crown on his pillow, Henry IV appears indeed to die; "he laie as though all his vitall spirits had beene from him departed. Such as were about him, thinking verelie that he had beene departed, couered his face with a linnen cloth" (3:57). The king's awakening to find his crown missing provokes no sharp exchange, only Prince Henry's explanation that "to mine and all mens judgements you seemed dead in this world" and his pledge to protect the kingdom against his father's enemies. The playwright, on the other hand, has added a tone of genuine distrust in Henry IV's charge against his son, and he has introduced a brassiness in Hal's response that serves as a chilling guide to his actions as king.

To the spectator or critic intent upon viewing the first half of the play as a depiction of Hal's robust youthfulness leading in time to remorse and a solemn acknowledgment of the responsibilities of kingship, the secondary action provides little more than comic relief; puerile material that "often degenerates into mere horse play,"[27] it does at least, we are told, allow the playwright to humanize the monarch.[28] To the commoner observing the action, on the other hand, it more likely functioned as a reinforcement of the social oppression and legal double standards depicted in the main plot. Of Hal's highway escapades, for instance, John Cobbler observes, "I dare not call [the prince] theefe, but sure he is one of these taking fellowes" (150–51). The clown Dericke, for another, is a walking parody of aristocratic disdain in his first appearance. Dressed in "silke apparell," he claims to have been robbed and threatens to have the law upon the watch (John Cobbler, Robin Pewterer, Lawrence Costermonger) unless they apprehend the culprit. Their plea to be spared provokes his taunt, "and you seeme to be poore men; therefore I care not greatly" (207–8), and his condescending snippet, "Tis a wonderful thing to see how glad the knaue is, now I haue forgiuen him" (213–15).[29]

At other moments the ironic counterpointing is more direct. Whereas Hal's robbery some would explain away in laughter as sowing wild oats, the thief (Cutberd Cutter), lacking the luxury of social position, must straightway be committed to Newgate for the same offense. Whereas Hal is released from prison within the hour, the thief must remain locked away until the sessions day. As Dericke and John comically reenact Hal's boxing the lord chief justice's ear, the point of social preferment is stressed again; *they* would not have hit a judge for twenty shillings since "there had bene no way but one with vs—we should haue bene hangde" (531–33). Later, the juxtaposition of the reconciliation scene between king and prince with the mock reconciliation between

Dericke and John (whose wife has dared to serve her guest "a dish of rootes and a peece of barrel-butter" [829–30]) tends comically to qualify both the seriousness and the sincerity of the former. In just such fashion Hal's final reconciliation with Henry IV moments before the king's death is qualified through the remarks of his cronies, Ned and Tom: "tis but with a little sorrowing, to make folkes beleeue the death of your father greeues you—and tis nothing so" (1015–17; see also 1000–1002). When they make the crucial mistake of calling Hal's bluff in public, they peremptorily are banished ten miles from the court. Even at this moment, in having Hal "abandon and abolish [their] company for euer" (1031–32), the playwright presumably intentionally omits the humanizing touch from Holinshed that the prince "banished them all from his presence (but not vnrewarded, or else vnpreferred)" (3:61).[30] That his friends are so obviously victimized for the sake of kingly image suggests that, for the Hal of the play, appearances are paramount; the political reality is far more significant than the spiritual.

In the second half of the play the subplot functions more directly to counterpoint Henry V's heroic exploits in France by foregrounding the grim underside of war. Below the surface reading that celebrates the national unity, as Jonathan Dollimore and Alan Sinfield observe concerning Shakespeare's play, foreign war, in practice, "was the site of competing interests, material and ideological, and the assumption that the nation must unite against a common foe was shot through with conflict and contradiction."[31] John Cobbler, his wife, and Dericke, for example, could care less about Henry's right to the French crown; their concern is only for the disruption of their life and livelihood. John's wife implores the captain not to impress her husband, who laments that he has "a great many shooes at home to cobble" (1219–20) and who weeps at the crass retort, "I care not. Thou shalt go" (1223). When Dericke's plea is rejected with similar curt disregard, he attempts to console the embracing couple with the quip that they are not so base-minded to die among Frenchmen; but then he ruefully adds that in such a situation no one knows whether he will be buried in a church. In any case, not the least semblance of patriotism colors the scene. Later in France, while Henry is obsessed with determining the location of the dauphin in the forthcoming battle so that he might gain revenge for the insulting gift of tennis balls, it is reported that his common soldiers are "sicke and diseased and that many of them die for want of victuals" (1380–82).

The same aristocratic mindset surfaces after the Battle of Agincourt in the report of English losses—the duke of York and the nameless "five or six and twentie common souldiers" (1601–2), a disregard compounded by Henry's eulogistic praise of the duke without so much as a word for the faceless foot soldiers. Two additional scenes, by forcing the spectator to view the action from the commoners' perspective, severely qualify the myth of a vaunted military victory achieved by the grandly heroic efforts of a nationally unified England. In both, harsh reality shatters romantic illusion. In one such scene Dericke, after much bombast, purposefully permits his French soldier to escape for fear of being killed himself in any further altercation; he further admits to staying clear of actual battle by fully half a mile through the trick of tickling his nose with straw to bloody his shirt in order to be sent behind the lines as a soldier in desperate need of rest and relief.[32] In the other scene Dericke and John Cobbler are seen looting on the battlefield; removing shoes and other valuable objects from the dead and dying—both French and English—they plan to make good their escape to England with their booty by disguising themselves as members of the duke of York's funeral party.

What traditional criticism has tended to regard as diversionary comic antics, then, some in the audience would more likely have viewed not as harmless folly but as trenchant satire. Perspective creates a similar bifurcation in the major action itself. Some of the spectators, to be sure, would have focused on the national heroics of Henry's leading his army to an astounding military victory over the arrogant and supercilious French. Against disease and overwhelming numerical odds he forges innovative battlefield strategy and an almost fanatical patriotism into a highly effective military machine. Beneath the fanfare, however, for the spectator so attuned, emerges a highly critical view of a society divided into self-interest groups and driven by a leader for whom national glory is synonymous with military conquest. For one thing, Henry's move against France is an act of raw aggression based on a claim to the throne traced back through four generations and espoused by the leading church official in England. If it seems ironic for the archbishop of Canterbury to counsel bloody war, one need look no further than Holinshed (and later Shakespeare) to discover that political interests dictate strange theological posturing. A bill, moved in the last parliament of Henry IV but not yet acted upon by the king, stipulated that certain lands held by the church—enough to maintain fifteen earls, fifteen-hundred knights, sixty-two hundred squires, and a hundred almshouses for relief of the poor—should be seized by the king for the good of the realm.

> This bill was much noted, and feared among the religious sort, whom surelie it touched verie neere, and therefore to find remedie against it, they determined to assaie all waies to put by and ouerthrow this bill: wherein they thought how to trie if they might moue the kings mood with some sharpe inuention, that he should not regard the importunate petitions of the commons. Wherevpon, on a daie in the parlement, Henrie Chichelie archbishop of Canturburie made a pithie oration, wherein he declared, how not onlie the duchies of Normandie and Aquitaine, with the countries of Anioou and Maine, were by vndoubted title apperteining to the king, as to the lawfull and onelie heire of the same; but also the whole realm of France, as heirs to his great grandfather king Edward the third. (3:65)

Neither Holinshed, the anonymous author of *The Famous Victories,* nor Shakespeare offers conjectures on whether Henry V was aware of the church's motive in urging the war; what is all too clear, though, is that the archbishop's interest conveniently serves the king's own ambitious designs and that the English commoners—who must bear the brunt of such an engagement—are simply caught in the middle. Whereas Holinshed stresses numerous actions undertaken by Henry ("diuerse good statutes, and wholesome ordinances, for the preseruation and aduancement of the commonwealth" [3:52]) in a parliament called immediately after his ordination, the playwright omits such material, depicting Henry's consideration of war as the first act of his reign. Also, whereas in Holinshed the dauphin's insulting gift of "Paris balles" precedes, and to some degree occasions, the war deliberations (3:64), the playwright pointedly defers the incident until Henry has determined for war, has rejected the French ambassador's offer of fifty thousand crowns annually and the hand of the Princess Katherine in marriage, and has pronounced that "all the crownes in France shall not serue me, except the crowne and kingdome it selfe!" (1118–20). Placed at this point in the action, the incident of the tennis balls merely provides Henry the opportunity to reiterate—and to justify on a purely personal level of pique—his predetermined posture of aggression: "in-steed of balles of leather we wil tosse him balles of brass and yron—yea, such balles as neuer were tost in France" (1149–51).

Throughout the entire sequence of events the spectator is forced uneasily to sense that Henry's view of the struggle against

France is not essentially unlike his view of the earlier escapades against the king's receivers at Gadshill. He may well claim, while on public display before the French king near the play's end, that his "comming into this land was not to shed blood, but for the right of my countrey" (1718–20), but his actions betoken an almost perverse pleasure in heavy-handed authoritarianism. Even his call to arms, for example, has a distinctly personal bias in his proclamation that "the proudest French-man in all France shall rue the time that euer these tennis balles were sent to England" (1170–73).

True to Machiavelli's observation that "there never was any remarkable lawgiver amongst any people who did not resort to divine authority,"[33] Henry, though clearly the aggressor, on several occasions glibly appropriates God to his side. At one point he defies the French as "open enemies to God" (1406); since the French herald has just claimed God for the French cause (1402), we are faced with that most despicable of political expediencies—the presumption that God is in both camps providing his blessing on the mass carnage and destruction that shortly are to ensue. A few moments later Henry exhorts his men to pluck up their courage; for, despite the ten-to-one odds, "God will defend you" (1520). Ironically, the only display of human affection in this part of the play is found in the French king's unwillingness to permit the dauphin to participate in the battle: "although I should get the victory, and then lose thy life, I should think my-selfe quite conquered" (1359–62). Since this one moment of genuine human compassion, in context, will prevent Henry's gaining personal revenge for the insulting gift of the tennis balls, it can be dismissed with disdain by the spectator inclined to view the action simplistically as a conflict between English heroism and French cowardice.

Nowhere is Henry's arrogance (or heroic assertiveness, depending upon one's perspective) more evident than in his relationship with Katherine of France. Having earlier rejected her as part of an offer to prevent his invasion of the land, he, as conqueror, now insists that, since he craves her, he "will haue her" (1775). When he abruptly informs her that he cannot spend half his time in wooing, her cool response signals that she is fully aware of her role as a political pawn: "I would to God that I had your Maiestie as fast in loue as you haue my father in warres!" (1796–98). The moment she exits he flashes his true colors with the ominous quip that, were he not certain of her father's goodwill in the match, "I would so rowse the towers ouer his eares that I would make him be glad to bring her me upon his hands and knees"

(1833–36). Perhaps his most brashly presumptuous remark is reserved for the end of the play: "I know, Kate, thou art not a little proud that I loue thee. What, wench, the King of England" (2002–4). In contrast, Holinshed records only that "it was concluded, that king Henrie of England should come to Trois, and marie the ladie Katherine" (3:113); the playwright himself has added the various exchanges that taint the English monarch with insensitivity, intolerance, and conceit.

The Famous Victories of Henry V, to conclude, can be viewed as either a glorification of monarchy or as an attack on its corruption, egocentricity, and militaristic monomania. Hal, from one perspective the mirror of Christian kings, is from another an impetuous upstart reflecting the worst of aristocratic disdain for his common subjects who is successful "because he alone embodies the contradictions that can bring disruption into the service of the state."[34] The crown—whether held by Henry IV or his son—in one view is the symbol of power and security, while in another it represents a force that is manipulative and acts disdainfully above the law without hesitation. If to some the play depicts a unified commonwealth, to others it reveals an oppressive oligarchy, with commoners subject to fear, suppression, and disruption of livelihood.

2
The Reign of Edward III

Published anonymously in quartos dated 1596 and 1599, *The Reign of Edward III* has been described as "one of the finest examples of the chronicle history plays,"[1] "the most academic and intellectual"[2] and the "most interesting and controversial" play in the Shakespeare apocrypha.[3] The association with Shakespeare dates back to Edward Capell in 1760, and subsequent critical arguments have been mounted both for his sole authorship (most recently by Wentersdorf, O'Connor, Hart, and Bell)[4] and for his role as collaborator or reviser (Muir, Kozlenko, Chambers, Ward, Koskenniemi, Mincoff, Leech).[5] The play also has been attributed in its entirety to others, most notably Peele and Kyd.[6] The date of the play probably falls somewhere between 1588 and 1596.[7] More certainty regarding the earlier date might, of course, strengthen the argument for Shakespeare's authorship or at least for a greater degree of artistry in comparison with other dramatic productions of the late eighties.

Traditionally, *Edward III*, we are told, is "a continuous illustration of warrior honor";[8] it "breathes the spirit of nationalistic feeling that was particularly strong in the years immediately after the victory over the Armada";[9] its real subject is "the national prestige in its steady progress from Crecy to Potiers and from Potiers to the conquest of Calais";[10] one of the "most ardent patriots, certainly, of his generation,"[11] its author effectively utilizes French history "as a foil to display the glory of English arms."[12]

Viewed in this light, the theme of the play is the education of a king who, in time, becomes a glorious ruler, a theme that extends as well—at least in terms of the heroics of war—to his son, the Black Prince. He who is to rule a country effectively must be able to rule himself, a lesson Edward painfully learns in overcoming and repudiating his lust for the countess of Salisbury; he also, with Queen Phillip's aid, must master his vengeful desire to annihilate his enemy and must learn that mercy and peace are attri-

butes of martial magnanimity. Edward, in a word, must learn
both publicly and privately that the king's law must subserve
moral law.[13] Just so, his son must learn independence in battle;
thrice his father refuses to send aid to rescue the Prince in order
to "season his [son's] courage" (3.5.39),[14] to require him to van-
quish death and fear "And ever after dread their force no more"
(55). Yet another theme, in such a view, reflects, in its depiction
of the limits of obedience to the king, the fundamental liberty of
the English citizen. Edward, in the face of the countess's threatened suicide, is ultimately forced to admit that he has no authority
over his subject's moral convictions, as is the French king when
he challenges the validity of his son's pledge of safe passage for
an English earl. Through such an experience, we are to suppose,
those in the audience corporately sense a "strong current of national feeling," a kind of "embodiment of England's glory"[15] as
they witness "a providential view of history in terms of the official
Tudor interpretation of earlier events"[16] from a playwright unmis-
takably "on the side of authority."[17]

As with *The Famous Victories of Henry V*, however, a spectator inclined to view the action from another perspective does not have
to search very far. One dominant characteristic of this society is
that individuals, acting as political and pragmatic policy dictates,
time and again publicly renounce loyalties or silently fail to ad-
here to previously stated principles. The impetus for Edward's
interest in France, for instance, comes in the opening lines
from Robert of Artoys, banished from France and newly created
earl of Richmond in England. His urging of Edward's right to
the throne—immediately following the conferral of his English
honors—can hardly be the act of high moral principle he claims:

> Perhaps it will be thought a heynous thing,
> That I a French man should discover this,
> But heaven I call to recorde of my vowes,
> It is not hate not any privat wronge,
> But love unto my country and the right
> Provokes my tongue thus lavish in report.
>
> (1.1.30–35)

He piously declares that his true duty lies in defiance of the
French king, John of Valoys, and in helping to secure the throne
for the "true shepheard of our commonwealth" (41). To the con-

trary, however, his fellow countryman, the duke of Lorraine, brands him a "Traytor" and a "viper" (107), his views as "poysoned" (119); and he must be physically restrained from attacking the renegade even in the presence of the English king.

That political expediency rather than principle dictates the action is suggested, as well, by precisely what Edward does *not* say. As the sole surviving descendent of King Phillip of Bew through his mother, Isabella, Edward must surely have had prior thoughts about his right to the French throne; yet he claims that his breast "was rakt in ignorance" (46) before Artoys's counsel. Now that he is aware of his right, he proclaims that those who resist his sovereignty will find their necks yoked with steel. Obviously, he considers the occasion of Artoys's pronouncement at court the opportune moment for asserting publicly his intention to expand the kingdom. It little concerns him that he, too, will be forsworn in the action, a point made explicitly clear in King John's later statement that Edward had joined with him in "solemne covenant" and that in moving against France the "fugitive" and "theevish" Englishman has "infringed [his] faith [and] / Broke[n] leage" (3.3.56, 57, 62–63). And there is yet another irony: When Edward violates his oath with France in order to declare war with that nation, he justifies his action as noble and righteous; but when King David of Scotland shortly thereafter violates his oath with England in order to declare war on that nation, Edward brands the action treacherous, tyrannical, and ignoble (1.1.28, 33, 40). Apparently it is not a matter of right and wrong but of convenience and political perspective. This same kind of political casuistry is evident in Prince Phillip's peremptory dismissal of Edward's claim to the French throne, *even* if it should happen to be valid: "bring he nere so playne a pedegree, / Tis you are in possession of the Crowne, / And thats the surest poynt of all" (3.1.112–14).

In only three instances in the play are characters true to their pledged word, and each case seems to reflect a fundamental incompatibility between honor and survival in this highly politicized stage world.[18] Warwick, for instance, gives his oath to perform any task whatsoever for Edward to remove the king's longstanding melancholy, only to discover that he has pledged himself to serve as pander to his own daughter. Only because the countess has the willpower to reject his counsel and preserve her honor does the earl retain a moiety of dignity and self-respect. Honor, however, is more costly for the Frenchmen, Villiers, and Charles, duke of

Normandy. Villiers, captured by the earl of Salisbury, "sweare[s] by [his] faith" (4.1.39) to procure for his captor safe passage through the enemy lines in return for his freedom; and he later insists that he must return to captivity unless Charles will honor the agreement:

> [I]n an othe we must be well advised,
> How we do sweare, and when we once have sworne,
> Not to infringe it though we die therefore.
>
> (4.3.41–43)

Charles, likewise, must subsequently argue the point with his father, threatening to fight no more if he cannot be "a soldier in [his] word" (4.5.97). In both cases the relationship of a subject's integrity to his allegiance to his king is the crucial issue. Villiers asserts that monarchic powers are limited, that he is not bound to obey a royal command that would encourage or bind him "Not to performe the covenant of [his] word" (4.3.34); King John argues the counterposition, that it lies in the king's power to affirm or revoke a subject's word and that no subject actually breaks his oath who "keepes it to the utmost of his power" (4.5.91). While in these instances Villiers and Charles prevail and are true to their word, the overriding irony is that both examples of such integrity form a part of a military disaster provoked by terrified French soldiers who interpret a solar eclipse as an omen of divine displeasure.

In at least three other instances loyalty is all-too-obviously for sale. Except for the French "cunning guide," who leads Edward through the shallow of the Somme River, the divisions of the English forces could not have joined for the decisive battle against the French; Gobin de Graie's reward is both freedom and "five hundred markes in golde" (3.3.1, 10). Similarly, the high rhetoric of political alliance—the aid and support that Bohemia and Poland have pledged to France "as league and neighborhood . . . when friends are in any way distrest" (3.1.42), 43)—quickly dissolves into the reality of "plentiful reward in Crownes, / That from [France's] Treasory ye shall receive" (51–52) and the promised division of the loot of battle. Even royal command assures no obedience when the spoil is a conquered Scottish king; John Copeland, in open defiance of Queen Phillip, drags his prey all the way to France to ensure his reward from Edward himself—knighthood and "five hundred marks a yeere" (5.1.101).

If the pervasive pattern of oath breaking and commercialized loyalties foregrounds a world of unprincipled self-seeking, the pattern of monarchic conduct is equally startling when one looks beyond the traditional view of the doting romantic lover who matures into an idealized political leader. Most importantly, Edward's lust for the countess of Salisbury endangers England's security. In hot pursuit of the Scots who have invaded his country, he vows with a "cheerful cry . . . [to] chase them at the heeles" (1.2.101–2). And, in anticipation of his own invasion of France, he has just dispatched Audley and his son, Ned, to levy soldiers, and Derby to solicit support from European allies. Action collapses precipitately on all fronts when he first sets eyes on the countess. The Scots scamper home unscathed, and Edward's military leaders are left in utter consternation. Derby's report that the emperor of Almaigne has agreed to join in league with him is met with confused mumblings, "Would it were the Countesse" and "Thou lyest she hath not" (2.2.28, 30); and Audley must stare in amazement as Edward peremptorily dismisses the charge of "horse and foote" (33) he has just organized. It is hardly likely that the line, "Lets leave him to his humour" (41), could have been delivered without a note of sarcasm bordering on disdain.

Moreover, various other characters call the spectators' attention to Edward's failures as a king. His confidant, Lodwicke, for instance, observes in an aside that Edward's blush in the countess's presence is that of immodest shame ("to waile his eyes amisse being a king" [2.1.17]), his paleness that of guilty fear ("to dote a misse being a mighty king" [21]). She herself accuses him of committing high treason against God in his desire to violate the marriage bond (2.2.261, 264) and later comments privately that this "corrupted judge" will tremble for his "packing evill" when called before the "universall Sessions" (165, 167, 168). Warwick, too, brands him a "doting King" (2.1.352); he concurs in his daughter's assertion that honorable death is preferable to a polluted life and specifically denounces Edward's sin as the abusive use of royal power:

> The greater man, the greater is the thing,
> Be it good or bad that he shall undertake.
> . . . .
> That sinne doth ten times agrevate it selfe,
> That is committed in a holie place,

An evill deed done by authoritie,
Is sin and subbornation.

(440–41, 447–50)

In this regard, Edward informs Lodwicke that because of his "greene . . . thoughts" his counsel house or cabinet will be a summer arbor, his estate her footstool; that which heretofore has been considered sin will now be deemed a virtue (65, 106, 116). Later, in France, John taunts Edward as "a belly god" given over to "tender and lascivious wantonnes" (3.3.159–60).

The numerous references to sinful conduct and neglect of political responsibility flatly confound any attempt by the perceptive spectator to pass off the incident as but an episode of Edward's salad days, a romantic flirtation from which he ultimately gains a sense of self-control. To the contrary, this strain of proud willfulness dominant in the affair of the flesh seems to possess Edward throughout the remainder of the play. For one thing, considering his earlier crass manipulation of moral values, one is prone to see his claim that God has directly aided him in his struggle against France as simply another example of self-serving arrogance:

Just dooming heaven, whose secret providence,
To our grosse judgement is inscrutable,
How are we bound to praise thy wondrous works,
That hast this day given way unto the right,
And made the wicked stumble at them selves!

(3.5.6–10)

If Prince Edward's later pronouncement that "heaven aides the right" (4.9.14) can perhaps be excused as a moment of youthful naïveté and patriotic exuberance, the father demonstrably has had far too much practice in the art of manipulating both the metaphysical and the human to permit such an assumption.

This same manipulative pride leads King Edward to a willingness to sacrifice his son's life in battle against the French. Determined that Ned will demonstrate his worthiness for knighthood, he refuses to aid the prince, despite successive implorations from Artoys ("Tis impossible that he should scape / Except your highnes presently descend" [3.5.15–16]), Derby ("oh succour him / Hees close incompast with a world of odds" [20–12]), and Audley:

Renowned Edward, give me leave I pray,
To lead my souldiers wher I may releeve,
Your Graces sonne, in Danger to be slayne.
. . . [H]e cannot free him selfe.

(27–9, 34)

Edward curtly denies Audley's request; in fact, he threatens death
to anyone who attempts to provide aid. His crass comment that
his son is laboring for a knighthood and that, should he die, "[w]e
have more sonnes / Than one" (24–25) smacks more of a fanatic
devoted to a heroic ideal than of a father/king concerned either
for the safety of his child, the proper lineal descent of his kingdom, or the outcome of the battle. And for those who make the
connection, there is a terrible irony in the fact that, in time, the
next in line to receive the crown—Richard II—will eventually
give it up without a fight. That Ned on this occasion fights
through to victory erases neither the irony nor the parental indifference. Indeed, it sets up an even more blatant irony in Ned's
thankful assumption in the final lines that his father ever "hath
bin his strongest shield" (5.1.226). Edward, in character to the
end, makes no effort to disenchant him.

Yet another motif that appears to undercut a grandly patriotic
reading of the play is the consistent depiction of the horror and
futility of war, regardless of the victor. For all the vaunted nobility
in Edward's and John's counterclaims of righteousness and
strength of purpose, war's true face surfaces time and again,
whether in Edward's flippant comment that his embracing the
countess of Salisbury in an unlawful bed is less sinful than "to
hacke and hew poore men" (2.2.123) or in French and English
taunts on the battlefield: Before John will resign the crown, the
"field shall be a poole of bloode, / And all our prospect as a
slaughter house" (3.3.120–21); the English power, in response,
will transform John into "one that teares [France's] entrailes with
[his] handes, / And like a thirstie tyger suckst her bloud" (124–25).
It is seen again in the fact that, of the forty men with Salisbury
who are granted safe passage by Prince Charles and ultimately
by King John himself, the great majority are slaughtered by the
time they reach Edward's camp. And it is seen when Ned—
surrounded, outnumbered, and expecting to face death at any
moment—concludes that life in such a world is idiotic and that
the "imperiall victorie of murdring death" is a sham; "to live or
die I hold indifferent" (4.4.158, 166).

Reports of actual combat center not on cause and principle but on the specter of agony and grisly death. A French mariner reports that the naval engagement prior to the English landing turned day to gloomy night:

> Purple the Sea whose channel fild as fast,
> With streaming gore that from the maymed fell,
> As did her gushing moysture breake into,
> The cranny cleftures of the through shot planks,
> Heere flew a head dissuvered from the tronke,
> There mangled armes and legs were tost aloft,
> As when a wherle winde takes the Summer dust,
> And scatters it in middle of the aire.
>
> (3.1.168–75)[19]

Edward subsequently threatens to destroy Calais with "fire and sword" (4.2.76), to "Put all to the sword, and make the spolye your owne" (5.1.11). When six wealthy merchants offer themselves as scapegoats for the city, his order that their bodies be dragged around the walls and then quartered is averted only by the queen's convincing him of the pragmatic value of mercy in leading the people to acknowledge him as king. His vicious side bursts forth again, less than two hundred lines later, when he vows to exact dire revenge for the presumed death of his son:

> [A]ll the Peeres in Fraunce,
> Shall mourners be, and weepe out bloody teares,
> Untill their emptie vaines be drie and sere.
> . . . .
> The mould that covers him [shall be] their Citie ashes,
> His knell the groaning cryes of dying men.
>
> (173–75, 177–78)

The spectators can conclude only that, if it served his purposes earlier to accept his son's presumed death with calm equanimity, it serves his purpose now to use such an event to justify a new round of general carnage.

Most significant, considering the multiple audiences of the chronicle play, is the plight of the commoner in this aristocratic world of conflicting political interests. While the members of the upper class would likely have seen nothing amiss in the casual references to the death of nameless and numberless commoners, many in the galleries and the pit, viewing such scenes as mere background for the actions of those who move society, would probably have been sensitive to the depiction of the bourgeoisie and the peasants as the real victims of the war in terms of both life and livelihood. One catches the note of disregard in Ned's report of battle casualties, as he carefully lists princes, barons, knights apart from the rest; even more revealing, the tabulation indicates one thousand commoners lost for every titled individual (31,000 to 211). Victims of a different sort are the "wretched patterns of dispayre and woe" (4.2.14), the "deseased, sicke and lame" (20), who, unfit to serve in defense of the besieged city, are forced out of Calais to save the expense of their food. Perhaps the most compelling view of the commoners' plight is a group of men and women fleeing from their homes with what possessions they can carry on their backs. They have no idea which side is winning; they know only that "envie and destruction is so nigh" (3.2.14) and that, whoever wins, their lives and sustenance are totally disrupted. Within moments, their worst fears are realized, as they hear reports that "Slaughter and mischiefe" are afoot and that the "unrestrained make havock" throughout the countryside (54, 55). Cities, cornfields, and vineyards are burning; many of the poor folk who escape the flames meet their deaths on the soldiers' pikes. Desolation is universal: "Here if you staie your wives will be abused, / Your treasure sarde before your weeping eies" (74–75).

Examined from the diametrically opposed perspectives of heroic patriotism and grim realpolitik, *Edward III* is revealed to be a play crafted to satisfy the demands of a highly heterogeneous audience. Like the other chronicle plays that thrived in the political climate of the last two decades of Elizabeth's reign, it served as a public forum combining entertainment with psychological release. Such drama depended in part on the sense of liberation that had been developed through association with the village green and holiday; at the same time it exercised a political consciousness born of the Renaissance, and it did so across the entire ideological spectrum. At that moment in English history, the chronicle play for the individual spectator—regardless of his or her particular social status or attitude toward the government and the state—functioned both as a festive occasion and as a vital political experience.

3

Sir John Oldcastle

Written and performed in 1599 and twice published in quarto form in 1600, *The First Part of the True and Honorable History of the Life of Sir John Oldcastle, the Good Lord Cobham* has received only scant attention, mostly as a Shakespeare curiosity concerning either the question of authorship or the question of the play's relationship to the forces that led him to alter the name of his infamous fat knight. Despite Shakespeare's name on the title page of Q2, the play's inclusion in F3 and F4, and Tieck's and Schlegel's claims that Shakespeare wrote the piece,[1] that point has been essentially settled by Henslowe's diary entry for 16 October 1599: "Receved by me Thomas downton, of phillipp Henchlow to pay Mʳ mundaye, Mʳ drayton & Mʳ wilsson & haythway for the first pte of the lyfe of Sʳ Jhon Ouldcasstell & in earnest of the Second pte for the vse of the companyy ten pownd J say receved."[2] Certainly *Oldcastle* seems to have been the Admiral's Men's response at the Rose, almost in shouting distance of the Globe, to the Lord Chamberlain's Men's production of *1 Henry IV*, though it is now impossible to determine whether the motive was the desire to capitalize on the popularity of Shakespeare's play,[3] envy of the rival company's success,[4] or an attempt "to reprove Shakespeare's company for treating disrespectfully the name of a Lollard martyr."[5] Nor is it possible to know whether the contemporary Lord Cobham, Henry Brooke, played any active role, though one recent critic would leave no doubt whatsoever: "Lord Cobham, in order to rectify the injury done [in Shakespeare's depiction of Oldcastle as a disreputable hanger-on of Prince Hal], induced the Admiral's Men to produce a long two-part play (of which only the first part is extant) narrating the 'true life' and martyrdom of the real Sir John Oldcastle."[6]

Even the small critical notice has been largely negative. If Schlegal believed *1 Sir John Oldcastle* deserves to be classed among Shakespeare's "best and maturest works"[7] and Harbage suggests that the quiet devotion of Lord and Lady Cobham is no less authentic than "the camaraderie of Hotspur and his sweet Kate, or the mutual regard of Brutus and Portia,"[8] the more common view is that "no member of the pseudo-Shakespearian group [is] more totally destitute of a single passage which might imaginably have been written by Shakespeare."[9] "Tiresome,"[10] "rousing, noisy, bawdy,"[11] the play is "a very indifferent composition."[12] Whatever might have happened in part 2, part 1 fails to make the hero interesting; Oldcastle appears to be "nothing more than an injured innocent."[13] Moreover, the "attempt to rival Falstaff in the character, Sir John of Wrotham, a thievish, rollicking, and gross hedge-priest, is as futile as it was daring."[14]

The bonus or "gefte" given by Henslowe to "Mr Mundaye & the Reste of the poets"[15] and the two quarto publications within a year of performance would seem to suggest that the play was reasonably successful. If so, it was able to hold the interest of commoner and aristocrat alike, the latter possibly even including Lord Cobham and his friends. Viewed in the traditional light, *1 Sir John Oldcastle* is broadly patriotic, capitalizing on widespread anti-Catholic sentiment and anti-French biases, and presenting a king who—reformed from the wild and lawless days of his youth—prepares to lead England into what the spectators well know history would record as an enormously successful invasion issuing in the capitulation of Charles VI and Henry V's political union with the French king's daughter, Katherine. Such a view reveals a mature king able to circulate expeditiously and knowledgeably among all ranks of English society, presumably in large part because of the earlier association with the likes of Falstaff and his cronies. Explicitly praising God for his deliverance from the assassins' scheme, he moves quickly to dispatch rebellion both among his peers and among the commoners. And, through it all, Sir John Oldcastle is portrayed as an individual fiercely loyal to the crown, a friend of the poor and needy, and a "protestant" who opposes the corruptions that permeate the church.

The depiction of the Catholic Church as the common enemy presumably would galvanize the opinions of an audience comprised of varied economic and political interests. More specifically, the bishop of Rochester, the ranking clergyman in the play, commits himself in act 1 to Oldcastle's destruction, and to this end he employs connivance, manipulation, and outright disobedience to the king. We first see him incensing the duke of Suffolk, a close confidant of Henry V, against Oldcastle and all of those who

upbraid the clergy;
Some carping at the livings we have,
And others spurning at the ceremonies
That are of ancient custom in the church.

(1.2.6–9)[16]

To encourage Suffolk to report this activity to the king and to gain support for arresting Oldcastle on the charge of heresy, Rochester—on behalf of the clergy—presents the duke a purse filled with gold coins. Moreover, moments later, when Henry questions the clergy's refusal to provide money for the wars in France, he is informed that they "have been very bountiful of late," trusting the king to consider them loyal subjects and to suppress "such malicious errors as begin / To spot their calling and disturb the church" (76, 80–81). The issue of monarchic authority surfaces when Rochester denies to Henry's face that individuals arrested on charges involving religion have the right of appeal to the throne; so, too, the issue of a subject's obedience to the king is foregrounded when—expressly in defiance of the king's orders—Rochester secretly dispatches orders for Oldcastle to appear before the ecclesiastical Court of Arches, an act that later provokes Henry's sharp rebuke:

Is this the duty you do bear to us?
Was't not sufficient we did pass our word
To send for him, but you, misdoubting it,
Or which is worse, intending to forestal
Our regal power, must likewise summon him?
This savors of ambition, not of zeal.

(2.3.76–81)

When by manipulation Rochester finally secures the king's signature on a commission to arrest Oldcastle, he swears that he holds in his hand "That which shall finish thy disdained life" (4.2.79).

If Rochester reflects the Machiavellian tactics of the church leaders, the parson and the summoner reflect the utter corruption of its ministers and agents. John of Wrotham, for example, privately assures the spectators that, with as many shapes as Proteus,

I am not as the world doth take me for:
If ever wolf were clothed in sheep's coat,
Then I am he, . . .
A priest in show, but, in plain terms, a thief.

(1.2.159–62)

Like the old Vice, he delights both in his villainy and in sharing it directly with those in the audience. A thief, a womanizer, a gambler—this priest who can "say a mass and kiss a lass" (2.1.248) moves from one sin of the flesh to another. When he robs the king himself and subsequently is forced to explain his wealth, he has the unmitigated gall to claim that the money has come from his skimming a portion of the tithes and offerings in his parish. The lampooning comments of Harpool, Oldcastle's aged servant, hint that such clerical malpractices are almost commonplace:

> I'll swear, drink ale, and fast Fridays with cakes and wine, fruit and spicery; shrive me of my old sins afore Easter, and begin new before Whitsuntide. (4.3.140–44)

Clum, the "sumner," also provides broad, satiric humor. Appearing at Cobham's house to issue Rochester's summons for Oldcastle to appear before the ecclesiastical court, he is forced by Harpool to eat the parchment, wax and all. Since his reputation for wenching apparently precedes him, Harpool threatens to make him eat, as well, the petticoat of any woman he disturbs within the diocese. In a further scene, while raiding Oldcastle's home, Clum exclaims with indignation that he can find "not a Latin book, no not so much as our Lady's psalter" (4.3.159–60); the Bible, the Testament, the Psalms—all are in English and must be committed to the fire!

Such an exposé of Catholic corruption could be expected to provoke an almost univocal response from the predominantly Protestant spectators. And the French involvement in the attempted assassination of Henry would capitalize on similar shared prejudices. Few in the audience fail to bristle when the agent Chartres pledges French support to Cambridge, Scroope, and Grey. The French offer of half a million crowns and countless troops obviously represents an attempt to ward off the English invasion. Henry's subsequent pledge that the French "shall dearly buy this villainy, / So soon as we set footing on her breast" (5.1.46–47) would warm the hearts of at least the more aggressive in the audience.

Once beyond the antipathies toward Catholics and the French, however, the strategies of the play are designed to reach out to all segments of the audience. The king, whose image is stained by a background of thievery and debauchery, prepares to invade France even while his English title is challenged from within. He, moreover, is engaged in a power struggle with the church that leaves the very nobleman who saves his life by revealing treason within the court an exile stripped of home and possessions.

Above all else, the play foregrounds civil unrest. Like the opening scene of *Romeo and Juliet*—in which the feud between the Capulet and Montague families builds with a steady crescendo through layers of servants, hotheaded youth, the patriarchs, and the prince himself—so in this play a feud between the households of Lord Powis and Lord Herbert refuses to be contained either by the sheriff of Herefordshire and a bailiff or by the mayor of Hereford, along with officers and townsmen. Even though the altercation is finally quieted by two judges, one must question whether it is the presence of more intimidating forms of civil authority or the fact that, with Lord Herbert receiving his fatal wound, the fight has reached a natural kind of stasis. In any case, these three successive waves of violence serve as an appropriate entrance into a kingdom in which peace at any level is a rare commodity indeed. Incredibly enough, in a play that on one level can be perceived as a glorification of national unity in an England led by a courageous, clever, and God-protected monarch, the spectators confront two rebellions, seven robberies, three fights, and one murder.

Once perspective has marginalized the theme of national harmony, what further emerges is a society in which law and justice simply do not prevail. The title figure undoubtedly provides the clearest example. According to the prologue, the drama will pay tribute to a "peer" "whose virtue shone above the rest," whose "true faith and loyalty" helped to support both "his sovereign and his country's weal" (8, 9, 10). In fact, though, as we have observed, Oldcastle is hounded throughout the play by the bishop of Rochester; he is—presumably erroneously—claimed as an ally by every rebellious group, and, at one point, the king himself becomes convinced of Cobham's treasonous activities, ordering Rochester to "take commission / To search, attach, imprison, and condemn / This most notorious traitor as you please" (4.2.74–76). Granted, he is fortunate enough to regain Henry's good graces and clever enough to escape Rochester's strategems for imprisonment and execution; nevertheless, at the end of the play, he and his wife have been dispossessed of their home and forced to take refuge in Wales with his friend, Lord Powis. And, if he is at least alive at the end of part 1, the spectators knew the fate of the historical Lord Cobham; presumably, the dramatic fate in the lost part 2 was the same for this nobleman described in the prologue as a "valiant martyr" (9).

In a word, Oldcastle—in the play, at least—is guilty of not one single criminal action, but even his knighthood cannot protect him from being victimized by the greed and guile of those around him. To make matters worse, those who pursue their own interests beyond the bounds of law go unpunished. Twice, for example, Rochester specifically disobeys the King and remains unscathed. On the previously noted instance of his defying the king's order by dispatching the summoner to arrest Oldcastle, Henry fully perceives the attempt "to forestal our regal power," snapping that such action "rather proves you malice his estate, / Than any way that he offends the law" (2.3.79–80, 81–83). Yet, for an act for which many would lose their heads, let alone their position and power at court, Rochester receives only the mild royal reprimand, "Go to, we like it not" (84). And Rochester does precisely the same thing at the conclusion of the play, ordering Oldcastle's arrest on the authority of the king's written commission, a commission that, sixty lines later, he heard Henry admit to be an act of misjudgment: "Pardon me, Cobham, I have done thee wrong; / Hereafter I will live to make amends" (4.3.136–37). The bishop, in other words, disregards Henry's recision, using the royal signature to negotiate Oldcastle's arrest and then flatly denying him the right of appeal to the throne. Again, for this utter disregard of the law Rochester remains untouched; indeed, in the final scenes his fortunes are as high as Oldcastle's are low.

Sir John, the parson of Wrotham, provides a less subtle illustration of the lawlessness of this society. Quite apart from his failures as a man of the cloth, he is obviously guilty of civil crimes in the highway robberies of Butler, of two clothiers, of the Irish rogue, Mack-Shane, and of Henry himself. He swears to his concubine, Doll, that "there's not a pedlar walks with a pack, but thou shalt as boldly choose of his wares, as with thy ready money in a merchant's shop: we'll have as good silver as the king coins any" (3.4.14–18). Caught for his robbery of the king when he later loses the gold coins in a game of chance, Henry orders him to be hanged for an example, yet within twenty-four lines releases him on the pledge of leading a reformed life. Likewise, when he admits his other crimes, he is ordered to Hereford for trial, but Rochester sends a letter to the judge on his behalf, suggesting that the parson's actions in exposing Mack-Shane as a murderer are grounds for exoneration. In the final scene, the judge of Assize berates him in explicit terms:

You stand attainted here of felony:
Beside, you have been lewd, and many years
Led a lascivious, unbeseeming life.

(5.11.25–27)

But, almost predictably, the judge pronounces that he is content
to release Sir John since "My lord of Rochester entreats for you"
(131), and the parson walks away totally free.

The same society that permits Rochester to operate above the
law and the parson to operate with impunity from within it strikes
others down with amazing celerity. None of the citizens, for example, who rise up in the name of religion, intending "no hurt
unto your majesty" (4.2.15), is given the opportunity of a trial by
peers. In the face of his earlier insistence to Rochester of the separation of the power of church and state, Henry's peremptory actions in snuffing out a pocket of religious discontent smack of
political opportunism. So, too, Cambridge, Scroope, and Grey—
the plea for pardon on their lips—are dragged to their death before they have a chance to explain the reasons for their action.
Perhaps to some of the spectators it is not so much a question of
whether they should be executed as it is their having at least as
much right to a hearing as a confessed murderer or highwayman.
After all, even Mack-Shane, unquestionably guilty of murder, is
afforded a trial before he is sentenced to be hanged. In brief, the
law in such a society seems whimsical both in style and application.

For those spectators inclined to look beyond the patriotic glitter,
it is in the king himself that the most sharply contradictory perspective emerges. From the various prose chronicles, from plays,
from poems, and from even a superficial knowledge of the past,
at least some in the audience would be familiar with the manner
in which the Lancastrians gained the throne, through usurpation
and murder. Certainly such knowledge renders highly ironic
Henry's several references to God's protection of the king. Also,
it might well explain his haste in summarily dispatching Cambridge, Scroope, and Grey without permitting them to speak. He,
to be sure, is fully aware of their motives; and the anonymous
playwright risks a lengthy and potentially boring passage lest the
point be lost upon the spectators.[17] Since Henry cannot deny his
father's usurpation of Richard II's throne, he obviously has no desire to have the matter debated in a court of law. By ordering the
rebels' immediate execution, he subordinates the law to his own
purposes even while he attempts to draw attention away from

both the political dimensions of this particular attempted assassination and from the larger issue of his right to the kingship by taking the aggressor's role in the invasion of France.

Henry's right to the throne is only the most fundamental of several ironies that reverberate through the play and that, for the spectators alert to them, form a pattern highly critical not so much of the principle of the monarchy as of the monarch's autocratic policies and qualities of leadership. Obviously, spectators sitting in the playhouse in the late 1590s could privately draw whatever analogies with Queen Elizabeth they desired. The dramatic strategies, in effect, encode such possibilities, depending upon the particular political agenda that the individual spectator brought to the playhouse.

Another irony is that Henry, through subtle waffling, emerges as the consummate politician, altering his values in accordance with the pragmatics of the moment. For one thing, various comments suggest that in his days antecedent to the play he has clearly prided himself in his ability to bridge the social gap and be accepted by his cronies as one of them; indeed, something of this same pride is reflected in his confidence in walking abroad at night in disguise and bantering verbally with the common citizens. Yet he appears insufferably arrogant when he confronts the citizen rebels, chiding Sir Roger Acton for tainting the gentry by condescending to "Join with peasants" and for degrading himself to their level by pandering to the passions of ignorant commoners (4.2.7–8). For another example, Henry at one point asserts that kingly prerogative extends no further than civil laws. He agrees with Cobham that his subjects' "conscience may not be encroached upon; / We would be loath to press our subjects' bodies, / Much less their souls" (2.3.18–20). Later, however, he demands total obedience from both body and soul, specifically insisting that he has the authority to dictate the constraints within which the conscience must operate:

> Thy conscience! then thy conscience is corrupt;
> For in thy conscience thou art bound to us,
> And in thy conscience thou shouldst love thy country:
> Else what's the difference 'twixt a Christian
> And the uncivil manners of the Turk?
>
> (4.2.10–14)

Such inconsistencies make it tempting to conclude either that Henry assumes that the law is relative or that he has no steady policy, whether from lack of conviction, courage, or intelligence.

The issue of Henry's rebellious youth also strategically cuts both ways in the play. If, to some observers, the focus is on his reformation and the experiential knowledge of human nature that he brings to the kingship, to others it is on a defect of personality in the prince that in sublimated form continues to plague the king. In such a view, Henry has never quite grown up. Not only does he continue openly to acknowledge his past activities; he seems to take an almost perverse pleasure in recalling them. Robbed in disguise, he remarks that the proverb has come true that "one thief robs another" (3.4.55). He wonders whether his old friends Peto, Poins, and Falstaff might not be around to help him, though he admits that the latter "is so fat, he cannot get on his horse" (57); and he notes almost boastfully to John of Wrotham that the "time has been I would have done as much / For thee, if thou hadst past this way" (62–63). Certainly Hal's reputation is legendary. Sir John claims that "the king should be good to thieves, because he has been a thief himself" (85–86). Hal, had Henry IV lived, would have "made thieving the best trade in England. . . . [H]e was the chief warden of our company. It's pity that e'er he should have been a king, he was so brave a thief" (102–3, 105–7). The dramatic irony admittedly provides a bit of humor, but the more significant point is that the king evinces no remorse or embarrassment for his reputation and offers no words of rationalization, either political or spiritual, for his past behavior. Instead, he quips, when informed that John had once been robbed by Hal, "[T]hen, thou art but even with him now, I'll be sworn" (95–96), and he later brags that "of old" he has "been a perfect night-walker" (4.1.20). At the very least, his choosing to wander at night in his old haunt in Westminister, to banter with John almost as if he were a fellow thief—and a bit later to win his money back in a game of dice—do nothing to enhance his image as a mature, competent ruler. Some spectators might well be led to wonder whether Henry has not simply transformed his thieving and dicing skills to a larger political arena.

If such a view depicts Henry as far from the ideal Christian prince of popular imagination, and the kingdom itself as rife with civil unrest, it also foregrounds a society in which the power structure exploits the masses. What the aristocracy would consider humor arising from the frantic efforts of a commoner to acquire noble rank, for example, the commoners would likely perceive as heavy-handed manipulation. More particularly, Sir Roger Acton searches out Master William Murley, the brewer of Dunstable—

no doubt because of his wealth—and informs him he has been elected a colonel of the rebel forces on the condition that he will provide a "great store of coin" (2.2.19). Flattered as an exemplary leader and assured that he will be knighted, Murley agrees to bring five hundred pounds, finally increasing the ante to ten thousand pounds if Acton promises to "remember my knight-hood and my place" (107). The moment the brewer exits, how-ever, Acton's aristocratic snobbery surfaces in the quip, "See what ambition may pursuade men to: / In hope of honour he will spend himself" (109–10). Later, Murley, utterly bedazzled by the thought of noble rank, orders his men to "follow your master, your captain, your knight that shall be" (3.2.3–4), and he carries with him a pair of golden spurs that he plans to wear at the cere-mony. Once Murley has produced his money and men, however, Acton will tolerate no mention of knighthood, snapping that the brewer talks of trifles and urging him on to battle. Henry's disdain is even sharper as he mocks Murley for his gold spurs and his horses "trapp'd all in costly furniture" (4.2.38); as the brewer faces death, there is something almost pathetic in his comment, "'twas knighthood brought me hither: they told me I had wealth enough to make my wife a lady" (34–36).

While Murley's exploitation results directly from his own mis-guided vanity, other signs of social oppression relate more di-rectly to the system itself. Elizabethan spectators, for example, might well find something familiar in the government's efforts to prohibit the freedom both of assembly and speech. Following the Powis-Herbert confrontation, a judge informs the sheriff that it is in the interest of the state and the commonwealth to suppress "all assemblies, except soldiers' musters, / For the king's prepara-tion into France" (1.1.112–13). There must be no meetings of any kind, and even the topics of conversation among the commoners must be monitored:

> When the vulgar sort
> Sit on their ale-bench, with their cups and cans,
> Matters of state [must] not be their common talk,
> Nor pure religion by their lips profan'd.
>
> (127–30)

Similarly, the king orders Cobham to "suffer [no] meetings to be had / Within [his] house" (2.3.24–5); later, he commands that the city gates be shut and "on the pain of death, / That not a citizen stir from his doors" (3.4.20–1).

The drama also suggests that in the power plays of a divided realm it is inevitably the common folk who suffer most severely. Murley, of course, is a case in point; as noted earlier, it is certainly no fiery zeal that costs him his life. His men appear to know even less about the larger issues of civil insurrection. Tom, for example, is only vaguely aware of the fact that he goes to fight against the church: "If it be, as I heard say, we go to fight against all the learned bishops, ... we shall speed ne'er the better" (3.2.34–35, 37). His concern is simply that he is likely to die. Since he is a bachelor, his friends may "scramble" for his goods; meanwhile, his friends Lawrence and Leonard "are making their wills because they have wives" (20–21). The commoners who fight for the king hardly seem to fare better. As two maimed soldiers and two old men beg at Cobham's door, one observes that "There be more stocks to set poor soldiers in, / Than there be houses to relieve them at" (1.3.3–4). Moreover, according to another, the poor have been ordered to remain within the parish, and the mayor of Rochester

> has set down an order forsooth, what every
> poor householder must give for our relief; where
> there be some 'sessed, I may say to you, had
> almost as much need to beg as we.
>
> (9–12)

Conditions are so severe that they would gladly crawl aboard ship to be slain in France rather than starve in England.

It would be misleading to argue that *1 Sir John Oldcastle* consistently advocates any specific ideology. To the contrary, the play appears to be politically eclectic. Cambridge bases his claim to the throne on a strict interpreation of the lineal descent integral to the theory of divine right; Henry V, like a tyrannous and ambitious stag, "gores the other deer, and will not keep / Within the limits are appointed him" (3.1.115–16). Murley, on the other hand, talks almost casually of making another king if Henry should be so unwise as to become involved in the religious struggle. Henry at times assumes a rigidly absolutist posture, affirming his power over the church and even the individual conscience; at other times he appears to acquiesce to the supremacy of both, lest he be a tyrant rather than a Christian king. Cobham, whatever his religious convictions, never wavers in his loyalty to the monarchy; to the king he owes "what is mine, either by nature's gift, / Or fortune's bounty" (2.3.9–10).[18]

I Sir John Oldcastle, in a word, is a play designed to succeed on the Elizabethan popular stage. While the censors and the aristocracy in general would probably have viewed it as a glorification of the monarchy and of England's imperialistic policy, others might well have viewed it as an exposure of a society gravely divided within itself and led by a morally flawed young Machiavel who promotes a war in France to cover dissension at home and his own questionable right to the throne. Oldcastle himself is the focal point of such a bifurcated response. In one view, he is a hero whose nobility, integrity, and generosity set him head and shoulders above the other figures; in another, he symbolizes the agony and injustice suffered by one in an unfavored minority and the helplessness of the individual who crosses the power structure in an autocratic society. If the play was designed specifically to counter the image of the historical Sir John Oldcastle as a fat, slovenly reprobate, and if it was commissioned by the powerful Henry Brooke, eleventh Baron Cobham, the supreme irony is that, while on one level it does just that, on another level it effectivley undermines the very social structures of which Elizabeth's contemporary, Lord Cobham, was so enamored and the efficaciousness of the relationship between his ancestor and the king which, apparently, he so jealously wished to guard.

4

Thomas, Lord Cromwell

The True Chronicle of the Whole life and Death of Thomas Lord Cromwell was entered in the Stationer's Register on 11 August 1602 and published later that year. "Written by W. S." on the title page led to the play's inclusion in F$_3$/F$_4$ and in the editions of Shakespeare from Rowe in the early eighteenth century to Hazlitt and Moltke in the nineteenth. While no one today argues for Shakespearean authorship, claims have included Thomas Heywood,[1] Robert Greene,[2] Michael Drayton,[3] George Chapman and Anthony Munday with revision by Thomas Dekker,[4] and Munday, Drayton, Henry Chettle, and Wentworth Smith,[5] the latter combination assuming an original two-part play condensed into the present text by Smith. At one extreme of critical estimation, August Wilhelm Schlegal declares it to be "not only by Shakespeare, but to belong, in my judgment, to his maturest and most excellent works";[6] at the other, Swinburne viciously attacks it as "utterly shapeless, spiritless, bodiless, soulless, senseless, helpless, worthless rubbish."[7] Subsequent criticism, if more restrained, is still divided,[8] but perhaps the most significant judgment lies in the general paucity of commentary.

In any event, *Thomas, Lord Cromwell* was apparently not a failure on the Elizabethan stage. That it was printed twice within eleven years suggests at least a mildly interested reading public, and the title page of each quarto notes that the play had been "sundrie times publickly Acted" by the Lord Chamberlain's Men (Q$_1$ 1602) and, following the change of name, by the King's Men, as well (Q$_2$ 1613). Perhaps, as R. B. Sharpe argues, the initial popularity was in part topical, in that through its whitewashing of Wolsey, it struck out at two Admiral's plays that blackened Wolsey and exalted Norfolk; in such a manner, Admiral's and Chamberlain's "were competing to show their parties' ancestors in the most favorable light."[9] Or, perhaps, the glorification of Cromwell, earl of Essex, was related to the Lord Chamberlain's Men's friendship with the ill-fated earl of Essex, Robert Devereux, and his faction.[10]

On the other hand, it is significant that the play never mentions Cromwell's gaining the title of Essex (or, for that matter, his appointment to the Garter and to the vice-regency). That omission, especially in light of the play's *de casibus* emphasis on his sudden fall from "highest fortunes" (chorus 4.1),[11] points strongly to the heavy hand of censorship. At the very least, Maxwell must certainly be correct that—far from "prov[ing] the freedom of the English theatre, in spite of censorship"[12]—it suggests the "better part of valor" was to omit anything that would directly foreground "the fall of another Essex."[13]

With its central figure a blacksmith's son who rises to political power during the reign of Henry VIII, *Thomas, Lord Cromwell* presents an interesting variation on the chronicle plays that focus directly on royalty. The traditional view is that the play depicts something of the excitement of a new social mobility in a recently reunited English society that is growing increasingly wealthy and powerful under a forceful king. Inspired by the "spirit of patriotism,"[14] it presents a "glorification of homely virtues"[15] with a protagonist who is "the very apotheosis of citizen virtue."[16] The opening scenes, for example, focus both on the industriousness of those in the lower-class and their ambition to develop the intellect as a means of improving their social standing. As Hodge, Will, and Tom speak with apparent enthusiasm of the need to be at work in the blacksmith's shop by five in the morning, young Thomas Cromwell chides them for disturbing his study:

> My books are all the wealth I do possess,
> And unto them I have engag'd my heart.
> O, learning, how divine thou seem'st to me,
> Within whose arms is all fidelity!
>
> (1.2.10–13)

Trusting that the time will come when gold will be but as trash to him, he proclaims that his birth will not deter him from realizing his ambitions. Old Cromwell, interestingly, is possessed of both values, on the one hand condemning his workers for loitering and threatening to throw his son out of doors for hampering their efforts, while on the other hand privately encouraging his son to pursue things of the mind. While Thomas's ambition is rewarded with the position of resident agent for English merchants in Antwerp, he soon yearns for the wisdom of travel and leaves for Italy. This experience, in turn, enables him, in Neopolitan disguise, to assist the earl of Bedford in escaping from his captors and, later, to aid Sir Christopher Hales in properly entertaining the lord chancellor, Thomas Wolsey:

> Thou art a man differing from vulgar form,
> And by how much thy spirit's rank'd 'bove these,
> In rules of art, by so much it shines brighter
> By travel, whose observance pleads his merit,
> In a most learn'd, yet unaffecting spirit.
>
> (3.3.9–13)

And Cromwell's dizzying rise to social prominence, an admittedly accelerated but not factually distorted reflection of history, includes appointment as solicitor to Wolsey, knighthood, master of the jewel-house, chief secretary to the king, membership in the privy council, lord keeper of the privy seal, and master of the rolls.

According to this interpretation, however, Cromwell never forgets his common roots. Indeed, three different incidents within a single scene underscore that point. Seeley, a poor man of Houndslow, and his wife, Joan, for example, have often fed Cromwell in the past when otherwise he would have gone to bed hungry; they assume that, "now that he is made a lord, he'll never look upon us" (4.2.19–20). Also, the Florentine merchant Frescobald, who earlier had given money to a young Cromwell in desperate need of it, now stands destitute himself before the lord chancellor. And, at the very moment Cromwell is hosting various dukes and earls, his old father, in farmer's gear, approaches, posing a potentially embarrassing reminder of his lowly heritage. Cromwell's response, though, both emotional and material, is immediate, as he publicly acknowledges his indebtedness to each:

> Here stands my father that first gave me life;
> Alas, what duty is too much for him?
> This man [Frescobald] in time of need did save my life;
> I therefore cannot do too much for him.
> By this old man [Seeley] I oftentimes was fed,
> Else might I have gone supperless to bed.
> Such kindness have I had of these three men,
> That Cromwell no way can repay again.
>
> (4.4.36–42)

The conclusion of the play, according to the traditional interpretation, stresses the modesty and the unstained virtue of this commoner elevated far beyond his aspirations. Following his arrest by the Council of Lords on trumped up charges of treason, he muses in the Tower over the irony that the greatness that provokes his fall came both "unsought" and "unlook'd for" (5.5.3). He glories in the friendship of the earl of Bedford, who attempted to forewarn him of his impending doom and who comes to bid him a personal, heartfelt farewell. His final advice to his young son is to neither fawn upon nor flatter fortune and to eschew ambition: "[L]et thy faith as spotless be as mine, / And Cromwell's virtues in thy face shall shine" (100–101). His peace made with heaven, he will escape this "land of worms" and rise to an "unmeasur'd height" when his "soul is shrined with heaven's celestial cover" (131, 132, 133). That Henry VIII's "kind reprieve" arrives mere moments too late tragically emphasizes that his death was the work of a designing few, not of the king he served faithfully and unceasingly.

Without doubt there were those in the audience who would have viewed Cromwell, from a markedly different perspective, as a commoner—"heart proud" and spirit "Too high indeed" (1.2.9)—who is an impudent upstart deserving of his fate. Indeed, to some spectators, Thomas's second soliloquy would be little less than revolutionary:

> Why should my birth keep down my mounting spirit?
> Are not all creatures subject unto time,
> To time who doth abuse the cheated world,
> And fills it full of hodge-podge bastardy?
> There's legions now of beggars on the earth,
> That their original did spring from kings;
> And many monarchs now, whose fathers were
> The riff-raff of their age.
>
> (71–78)

They would note, as well, the sheer effrontery of Thomas's vow to "build a palace where this cottage stands / As fine as is King Henry's house at Sheen" (57–58) and his apparent obsession with the excitement of unlimited ambition and power:

> for time and fortune
> Wears out a noble train to beggary;
> And from the dunghill minions do advance
> To state and mark in this admiring world.
>
> (78–81)

He pointedly observes that Wolsey's origin, too, was mean, "a butcher's son" (88). Later, in a similar spirit, Cromwell disdains his mercantile position in Antwerp, branding it "plodding . . . trash" (2.1.2, 5) as he determines that travel is needed to better his mind. And, of course, his experience pays off—but not so critically as his willingness to say what is expected (when in 3.3 his lugubrious praise of Englishmen—compared to the lust of the French, Italians, and Spanish and the riotousness of the German and Dutch—gains Wolsey's attention and his initial preferments) and to do what is expected (when in 4.1 he readily turns over Wolsey's private papers and thereby secures for himself a knighthood and King Henry's personal favor). His deference to his social superiors is nowhere more graphically obvious than in his willingness to use his father's servant, Hodge, as a decoy so that the earl of Bedford might escape captivity.[17] Admitting the danger that "this simple wretch" might be tortured or killed, he proclaims that it is better that the commoner Hodge "live in thrall, / Than such a noble earl should fall" (3.2.101, 104–5). Most heinous of all, the spectators learn later in the play that Cromwell, in order to work Henry's will, has circumvented the law itself by devising the scheme that parliament has the right to condemn an individual to death without the benefit of public trial.

For spectators inclined by status to resist a high degree of social mobility, such a pattern of self-serving actions in the wake of his earlier vow "to flourish and control" (1.3.91) renders as little more than posturing Cromwell's claim moments before his death of spotless faith and virtue (5.5.100, 101). Many would probably be far more inclined to believe, with Bagot, that Cromwell but speaks what he would have others hear, that he full well realizes that the only way to assure himself of profit and advancement is to "lie, cog with his dearest friend, / And as for pity, scorn it" (2.2.48–49).

Either view of Thomas—whether that of the heroic overachiever or that of the time-serving scoundrel—assumes a spectator who endorses a hierarchical society, albeit one with a degree of social fluidity, and a monarch whose near-absolute power is evident even in his physical absence. The strategies of the play suggest further, however, that for some in the audience the stage served as a scathing attack upon such a society. Indeed, in almost one-third of the scenes, Cromwell does not even appear, and in several he is not the subject of conversation. What the play foregrounds above all is a society in which law and order are at worst a sham and at best a device for privileging the aristocracy. Social mobility—for some, more accurately, social mutability—is in most instances little more than a desperate and sometimes pernicious effort to cater to and enjoy the pleasures of the privileged class. Thomas's pride of intellect, for instance, and his eagerness through serving those above him in station to gain increasingly high preferment are shadowed more odiously in the actions of the vicious social riser, Bagot. This "damned money-broker" (1.3.57), a "cannibal, that doth eat men alive!" (62), is determined to destroy Bannister, his father's master. At the same time, by ordering the arrest on behalf of the Italian, Frescobald, he expects to gain liberal remuneration. When he receives repudiation rather than reward, he next purchases jewels that he knows to "be stolen" (2.2.14), then attempts to sell them in Antwerp at an enormous profit. This scheme—as it turns out—has earlier involved a robbery of the king's treasury and consequently is disastrous for Bagot, who loses both his wealth and his freedom. While he is never seen or heard of again after act 2, his presence early in the play serves to deflate any grand assumptions of a society with genuine class mobility. Bagot's methods are simply too obvious, and those above him in social status refuse to condone his efforts to rise in station; Thomas, on the other hand, serves the purposes of the aristocracy, and his advancement results not so much from innate ability and intelligence as from his ability to be useful to his social superiors. The foil relationship of Cromwell and Bagot, in a word, sharply delimits any sense of freedom and equality; the commoner may safely aspire to wealth and grandeur only to the extent that he can be controlled and exploited by those above him.

It is also a society riddled with class divisiveness and violence, whether the petty thievery, during the channel crossing, of the watermen who steal Hodge's food while he is seasick (2.3) or the organized criminal band that robs Hodge and Cromwell in Italy (3.1). Certainly few commoners were likely to miss the irony in Cromwell's remark to his servant, as they stand stripped of valuables on a bridge in Florence, "Hodge, I believe thou must work for us both" (27–28); Cromwell's emphasis on things intellectual has obviously made him ill-prepared to survive at the level of the working masses. Nor would they be unresponsive to Hodge's quip that those called the banditti in Italy would be considered "plain thieves in England" (38). Once the two have been rescued by liberal gifts from Frescobald, he quips further, "[L]et's keep our standing upon this bridge; we shall get more here, with begging in one day, than I shall with making horse-shoes in a whole year" (105–7). Similar social sarcasm surfaces in the following scene as Hodge, disguised as the earl of Bedford, "feel[s] honor come creeping on!" and thus assumes a most "gentleman-like" pose of melancholy (3.2.113–14, 115). He proclaims that the fleas that normally pester him will "dare not meddle with nobility" (123–24), and he writes pompously to friend William, "I am not as I have been. . . . I do commend my lordship to Ralph and to Roger, to Bridget and to Dorothy, and so to all the youth of Putney" (138–39, 141–43). That he is shortly thereafter released as worthless—in comparison with the aristocrat for whom he is a surrogate—merely exacerbates the social divisions as it turns the satire in the opposite direction. Moreover, if the spectator can assume that Hodge is consciously mimicking the aristocracy throughout this scene, such hardly seems to be the case in 4.2 when, now servant to Sir Thomas Cromwell, he assumes the very snobbery he has earlier derided. His presumptuous order, "away with these beggars here" (36), prompts Old Seeley's retort, "you, Hodge, we know you well enough, though you are so fine" (41–42). Far more poignant is the plight of Bannister's family when he is arrested for debt. His wife laments that they "scarce have meat to feed our little babes" and swears, should her husband be set free, that they will eat only "one meal a day; the other will we keep, / And sell, as part to pay the debt we owe" (1.3.65, 71–72).

By emphasizing such class division and oppression, the playwright forces the spectators to confront a stage world characterized not by a sense of pride in unity but by blatant efforts to gain self-gratification and a social hierarchy that utilizes a sense of mobility as, in effect, a strategy of containment. Nowhere is this more obvious than in the factors that lead to Cromwell's fall. Admittedly, the lord chancellor, responsible for abolishing Catholicism from England, every Catholic in the audience would deem a hypocrite for whom temporal execution is but a prelude to eternal damnation. His attack on the church draws the special wrath of Stephen Gardiner, bishop of Winchester, who pronounces that "religion's wronged":

> The infant yet unborn
> Will curse the time the abbeys were pull'd down.
> I pray now where is hospitality?
> Where now may poor distressed people go?
> . . . .
> Where religious men should take them in,
> Shall now be kept back with a mastiff dog.
>
> (4.2.84–86, 90–91)

On the other hand, most spectators shared a strong anti-Catholic bias, in part, as David Bevington has noted, because "popular sentiment feared that much of the court was drifting back toward religious conservatism or outright Catholicism."[18] Such spectators would have been delighted with Cromwell's declaration that he has abolished the "antichrist" and "popish order" from the land:

> I am no enemy to religion.
> But what is done, it is for England's good.
> What did they serve for, but to feed a sort
> Of lazy abbots and of full-fed friars?
>
> (4.2.75–78)

And this prejudice would simply have compounded their readiness to view Gardiner as the archvillain of the piece. Indeed, the church is merely a convenient front for his attack, a point clearly established in a soliloquy in which he admits that his personal envy breeds with Cromwell's promotion to the lord chancellorship: "I fear this climbing will have sudden fall. . . . Shall Cromwell live a greater man than I?" (4.1.69, 73). After suborning two henchmen (whose lives he had saved from a just sentence of death) to testify that they heard Lord Cromwell threaten the king's life, he does not hesitate to appropriate the power of the church to legitimize his treachery:[19]

> Kneel down, and I will here absolve you both:
> This crucifix I lay upon your heads,
> And sprinkle holy water on your brows.
>
> (4.5.30–32)

Promising them heaven's grace for this meritorious deed, he single-handedly orchestrates Cromwell's downfall as he subsequently convinces members of the Privy Council—through execution without trial—to hoist the lord chancellor on his own petard.

Gardiner's actions against Cromwell, by demonstrating the precariousness of political appointment for a commoner, above all expose social mobility as more delusion than reality. Even Lord Bedford, who owes his life to Cromwell, fails in the face of peer pressure to act decisively to avert his friend's disaster. For one thing, in a personal encounter with Cromwell and his train, he allows the lord chancellor twice to walk away without insisting that what he has to say is a matter of life and death. For another, he sends a letter to Cromwell but without any external mark of urgency that would prompt the lord chancellor to read it without delay.[20] All too obviously, he is not willing to do anything to save Cromwell that will unduly attract the attention of his fellow lords. In the scene of the arrest itself he stands passively to the side, uttering only the single comment that he is grieved at the sudden fall. Moreover, his comment before Cromwell enters ("Amen, and root thee from the land! / For while thou livest, the truth cannot stand" [5.2.9–10]), spoken moments after the proclamation of treason, is highly ambiguous. If it is not intended, as an aside, to refer to Gardiner as the perpetrator of the dishonest charge, it is a palpable public effort to curry the favor of his fellow lords, all of whom support the arrest.

Interestingly, Henry VIII never appears on stage, although, as Ribner observes, he is "felt" as an "unseen but inexorable power whose relations to his victims, though not at all clear, are above scrutiny, much less criticism."[21] For those spectators attuned to the scenes that marginalize the patriotism and the heroics of Cromwell's rise to power, the play by implication is certainly a denunciation, at the very least, of this particular monarch. With the falls of Wolsey and More as backdrop, the court is depicted as a web of intrigue in which the ruler appears to play one favorite off another in order to maintain his absolute power. In this regard Cromwell, like those before him, is simply one whose usefulness has been served. If the play spares him the historical indignity of a letter to an indifferent monarch, mawkishly pleading for his life, it makes its point even more incisively by departing from the factual record that Henry failed to respond in any fashion. For, in a sense, Henry's unhistorical reprieve, a response in the play to Cromwell's notification of his arrest, is the final insult. If the king was aware of the situation and timed his response to arrive moments too late, thus putting the best royal face on the death of his chief officer and leaving others to assume the blame, that is at least an act of chicanery in the service of political prudence. If he indeed did know nothing of what was going on in the highest political circles of his court, and his lord chancellor was executed without his knowledge, the even bleaker conclusion is that he should have known. And, at the very least, one must asume that he would strike out with rage against those who perpetrated the action without his permission. Without such a response one must logically infer that Henry was privy to the action and that his reprieve is merely a ploy. Or, if the play would have the spectators believe the king is unaware of the assassination, they must also assume an absolutism involving an incredible indifference at the highest level to the human dimensions of his political power.

It is a society from which the worst dimensions are reified in the observations of a common citizen near the end of the play—on the one hand, the patronage system and self-interest at their worst: "All that I have, I did enjoy by him: / And if he die, then all my state is gone" (5.4.10–11); on the other, the monarchic system at its most corrupt: "He that in course secure will keep himself, / Must not be great, for then he is envied at" (17–18).

5
Edmund Ironside

Edmund Ironside, a Tudor chronicle play preserved as the fifth of fifteen plays in the Egerton Manuscript 1994 in the British Library and first edited by Eleanore Boswell in 1928 for the Malone Society, has gained fresh attention through Eric Sams's edition in 1985 as *Shakespeare's Lost Play.* The date of 1647, assigned by James Halliwell-Phillips,[1] has been refuted on every reasonable ground, and critics generally have placed the drama somewhere between 1590 and 1600.[2] Sams, resurrecting a claim advanced in 1954 by Ephraim B. Everitt in *The Young Shakespeare: Studies in Documentary Evidence*, conjectures that *Edmund Ironside* is a work of Shakespeare's juvenilia, written for the Lord Admiral's Company, with the role of Edmund—requiring a physically large person—ideal for Edward Alleyn.[3] He settles on early 1588 and argues that *Ironside* is the "very first chronicle history and hence in its own right a work of seminal significance in the history of English and World drama.[4]

Such statements are designed to stimulate response, as is the book as a whole. On certain matters Sams argues persuasively, for example, the relationship of the role to Alleyn and the probability that the lost *Hardicanute*, owned by the Admiral's Men and played by them as late as 1597–98, was a sequel to the play; he also carefully traces the journey of the manuscript through ownership by the William Cartwrights, father and son, to Dulwich College, to Dublin and the estate of the second earl of Charlemont, and, finally, to the British Library in 1865. On the central matter of Shakespearean authorship, however, his argument is likely to convince only the converted. He explores at length the "comparative absence or paucity of certain literary devices"[5] and the presence of others in Shakespeare's work and *Edmund Ironside*, comparing also the imagery, the vocabulary, the modus operandi, and specific verbal affinities with *Titus Andronicus*. His conclusion is that Shakespeare "either plundered [*Edmund Ironside*] or he wrote it";

since he was "no such wholesale plagiarist" but often did "thriftily re-use . . . his own phrases and ideas,"[6] the deduction should be clear. Most unfortunate, along the way, is a certain belligerence in Sam's attack on what he describes as "the transparent confusion and inadequacy of current Shakespeare studies"[7] and on the inherent difficulties, regarding the Shakespeare canon, of "get[ting] past those self-appointed guardians of the gate-way, the professed and professional sceptics."[8]

While Sams could no doubt justifiably claim that such a brief synopsis fails to do justice to a thesis that he develops over the course of two hundred pages, my purpose here is not, directly, to argue one position or another in the authorship controversy, but instead to consider what might be gained through an examination of the dramaturgical quality of the play itself. Both Boas[9] and Boswell[10] describe its importance as a dramatization of Anglo-Saxon history, and M. Hope Dodds notes, in passing, the author's "distinct idea of character drawing."[11] On the other hand, comments that the play is "totally devoid of structure,"[12] "outstanding only in its inartistic utilization" of popular conventions,[13] that the author, "with no constructive skill,"[14] "deserves his oblivion,"[15] seem, at the very least, to demand qualification. Of primary significance is the play's relatively complex dramatic perspective, structurally combining something of the Vice/hero-villain who, center stage, shares his Machiavellian schemes privately with the spectators, and something of the conflict of mighty opposites, two carefully balanced figures who command equally the attention of the audience. More specifically, three characters—Canutus, Edmund, and Edricus—dominate our attention, delivering 61 percent of the total lines in the play. The title figure, Edmund, speaks 13 percent; Canutus, 22 percent; and Edricus, 26 percent.

The action focuses in large part on the rivalry between the two kings, "the patriot English king and his great Danish rival,"[16] both of whom, as mighty warriors addressing their followers, establish a fundamentally sympathetic rapport with the spectators in the opening act.[17] Canutus, more specifically, describes himself as Edward's sovereign, proclaiming that his father's conquest and his own election by English "lords spiritual and temporal" (11)[18] established him as "heir apparent to the crown / When Ethelredus lived" (16–17); and the archbishop of Canterbury, along with various English noblemen, duly affirms his claim, acknowledging his election "for public profit of the realm / for peace, for quiet and utility" (28–29). He, moreover, initially appears kingly in deed as well as title.[19] Readily granting a request that he establish his court at Southampton's castle, he immediately faces the choice of controlling the unruly Englishmen through tyrannical oppression, as Edricus advises, or through moderation, as his general, Uskataulf, counsels. Without hesitation he opts for the latter, stating that he will "so moderate himself" that

> Englishmen shall think me English-born.
> I will be so mild and gentle to my foes
> If gentleness can win their stubborn hearts.
>
> (213–15)

So, too, Edmund in act 1 is established as a courageous and magnanimous leader concerned for the equity of payment and food for his soldiers. The arrival of Leofric, earl of Chester, and Turkillus, duke of Norfolk, driven by "remorse of conscience" to return to their true English king and to plead for Edmund's mercy, tends further to reinforce the spectator's sympathy for the English ruler. At the same time, any disdain for Canutus is mitigated not only by the fact that the two English lords are twice forsworn but also that they now callously leave their children as inevitable victims to the Danes. Moreover, Edmund's greeting, for the audience, at least, is tinged with ambiguity. His comment that their return gives him more joy than Agamemnon's at the conquest of Troy no doubt stirs recollections of the Greek's tragically short-lived felicity upon his return to his homeland; and the claim that England shall never fall until her own sons prove false (a cliché used for similar effect in *King John*) is doubly ironic, both in that Turkillus and Leofric have indeed already been traitors to their native land and in that the spectators view the scene with a knowledge not only of the extensive internecine strife that was to come in the fifteenth century but also of the successful Norman-French invasion that awaited England just beyond Edward's reign.

Edmund and Canutus, then, are established as double protagonists in the opening act; and, as the head-title, "War Hath Made All Friends," suggests (*Edmund Ironside* is actually only a label on the outer cover), the final resolution of the action basically reaffirms this situation. Throughout the play, though, the playwright heightens dramatic interest in their conflict by alternately manipulating the spectators to a response of admiration and disdain for both men. In act 2, for example, Canutus's "strictly honorable"[20] wooing and winning of an English queen in Egina, Southampton's daughter, tends to provoke a greater degree of sympathy, as does his perception and denunciation of Edricus as a double-dealing villain:

> Gross flattery, all soothing sycophant
> doth blind thy eyes and will not let thee see
> that others see thou art a flatterer.
> Amend, amend thy life, learn to speak truth.
>
> (2.3.799–802)

On the other hand, the spectators view with disgust the Dane's willingness in a later scene to be a party to Edricus's scheme falsely to insinuate himself back into the favor of Edmund in order to betray the English leader at a critical moment in battle (3.4), and the audience can only be horrified at Canutus's flagrant cruelty in ordering and then personally overseeing the mutilation of Leofric's and Turkillus's sons, each of whom suffers the amputation of hands and nose for his father's political betrayal. Edmund, likewise, gains greater admiration through his courage and perseverance in the various battle scenes in act 3, claiming in scene 4 that God fights with him and graciously praising leaders and common soldiers alike. The spectators can react only with disdain, however, when Edmund proves hopelessly gullible to Edricus's machinations in act 4.[21] That Edmund rips off Edricus's disguise—condemning "cursed treachery" in the name of "Policy" and praising God for exposing the "smooth-face forged tale" (2.1364, 1365, 1373)—makes it all the more incredible that in less than fifty lines he repudiates the warning of his general and accepts the fellow as a trusted ally:

> I pardon thee for all
> and will reward thee with deserved grace.
> I will not doubt it, faith, I think 'tis true.
> . . . .
> I mean indeed to credit thee
> by being captain-general of my army.
>
> (1418–20, 1423–4)

Even worse, after Edmund has been betrayed in battle and has narrowly escaped capture and after he has branded Edricus an "incarnate Devil" and a "Judas" (5.1.1617, 1644), he yet again displays "credulous trust"[22] in falling victim to Edricus's flattery and Falstaffian distortions of battlefield conduct, confirming his love for the turncoat and his intention to honor him for his loyalty (1731–33). In the final scene, however, both figures, Edmund in victory and Canutus in defeat, once more gain a degree of sympathy from the spectators. Each restates his claim to the throne, and the two kings then face each other in protracted but indecisive single combat. When Canutus yields to Edmund, offering either his hand with "friendship firm, immovable" or his sword with "enmity irrevocable," Edmund embraces him as a "war begotten friend"; and the two, "surfeited with woe and war," pledge to strive to see who "by mutual kindness" shall best deserve to "be termed a friend" (5.2.2001, 2002, 2008, 2009).

The author is able to develop and maintain this swinging ambivalence toward both principals in part because of a lack of psychological depth in either of them. The spectator is given no clue, for instance, concerning the truce by which Edmund, after fighting with Canutus throughout the play and finally gaining the clearly superior military hand, suddenly offers "like friends [to] consult / upon partition of this noble isle" (5.2.2039–40). Are the opposing leaders buying time until the opportune moment to violate the agreement? Does one or the other actually fear defeat and perceive the negotiated settlement as the best that can be salvaged? Without the slightest hint of any such compelling political motivation, the spectator, at least at first glance, is forced to infer that the war-weary lords are motiviated by a magnanimity of spirit strong enough to cast aside both personal and nationalistic aspirations. In much the same way, the spectator, in the absence of any other motivation, must assume that Canutus falls in love with Egina and desires to marry her. If there is a political plan to weld English and Danish stock, it is never mentioned. And surely the attraction is more than mere lust, which the Danish leader could presumably have satisfied without resort to the clergy. Similarly, beyond the fact that it gratifies the earl's request, we know nothing of any political motives behind Canutus's decision to establish court at Southampton's castle. Then, too, is there some unspoken reason for Edmund's unquestioning forgiveness of Leofric and Turkillus or for his twice, not merely forgiving Edricus, but entrusting him with power? What motivates Canutus to strike out against Edricus's villainy at one moment and then to embrace him as a military ally the next? Admittedly, some of the political or personal concerns might have been made manifest in a second play, but in the play as we have it the playwright consistently forces us to remain outside the characters and to deal with them only as highly stylized individuals.

This superficiality of characterization is the more remarkable when set alongside the psychological complexity of Edricus, the third principal figure. Indeed, that Edricus appropriates all villainy unto himself is central to the author's ability to maintain a fundamentally positive rapport between the spectators and the opposing warriors. This duke of Mercia, a "Vice advanced to villainy" belonging "half to Holinshed, half to homiletic allegory,"[23] is the only significantly internalized character, delivering nearly one-third of his lines in seven soliloquies and four asides. Such lines function as explanation rather than perturbation, providing the opportunity for announcing rather than contemplating his future deeds. Even so, in his private comments to the spectators, Edricus shares his machinations against both Canutus and Edmund, how he literally plays one against the other; and in doing so, he also establishes a pattern of anticipation in the spectator that the ensuing action fulfills.

Of primary significance, Edricus is the only psychologically real character on the stage, a living creature among automatons whose creed is to survive and thrive by whatever means necessary:

> My state may be compared unto his
> that ventures all his credit and his wealth
> upon the fickle hazard of a die.
> The crown I level at, I venture life
> the dearest jewel and of greatest price
> that any mortal hath possession of.
>
> (3.5.1142–47)

Clearly his allegiance is only to self; as Spivack observes, he "puts himself into danger to display his dexterity in getting out of it."[24] If he prefers Canutus to Edmund, it is only because the Dane is unaware of his past, whereas Edmund's knowledge of the fact that Ethelred raised him from the position of a ploughman's son to a dukedom galls and embarrasses. Nevertheless, the practiced villain is prepared, whatever the outcome:

> Mass, if [Edmund] do, and fortune favour him
> I will so work as I'll be in his grace
> and keep my living and myself unhurt
> but if Canutus chance to gain again
> then I am his, for I can gloze with all.
>
> (1.2.311–15)

He prides himself in his ability to "play an *Ambodexter's* part / and swear I love, yet hate him with my heart" (330–31). Similarly, in act 5 he describes his ploy to encourage the two leaders to engage in single combat as the "Fountain of wit, the spring of policy, / the flower of treason and villainy" (2.1844–45); the key ingredient is again his own security:

> [W]hosoever hath the better, yet shall I
> be gracious in his eye, as who should say
> I was causer of his victory.
> Besides, I shall insinuate myself
> into the bosom of opinion
> and be esteemed my country's buckler.
>
> (1851–56)

When, much to his displeasure, the play ends in peace and reconciliation between Canutus and Edmund, Edricus notes in an aside that, as soon as "occasion fits" and safety permits, he will "be revenged on both" (2056, 2061).

Nowhere is Edricus's crass egocentricity more repugnant than in his mistreatment of his poverty-stricken family in act 2. Flatly denying his parentage, he brands his stepfather a "whoreson cuckold," "slave," and "dolt" (2.492, 493) for failure to acknowledge him as a duke and denounces his mother as an "old hag, witch, quean, slut, drab, whore and thief" (501). While he agrees to accept his stepbrother, Stitch, as his chamberlain, he immediately begins to instruct the fellow on how to "creep into opinion by deceit" (522); and the first thing the servant is forced to do to prove his loyalty is to bludgeon the parents, stopping only when they are "whipped out of town" (533).

Through establishing a private level of communication with the spectators, Edricus also acts as a diabolic guide to the events of the play. The entire second scene consists of a soliloquy in which he shares with the audience his pride of position and his unholy delight in his ability to dissemble, to "cloak, cozen, cog and flatter with the king / crouch and seem courteous, . . . in all things use deceit" (290–92). Later, in composing a letter in which he pleads for Edmund's forgiveness, he revels in the use of a plain style as a cover for deceit; his "rare-conceited piece of work" (3.5.1200) and his disguise as his own messenger are "experiments of matchless policy" (1239) worthy of his "wit." And success only further reveals the perverse pleasure in his sense of superiority: "See what dissimulation brings to pass / how quickly I can make the

king an ass" (4.2.1426–7). He literally is at the center of each
major turn of events, and in every case he shares with the spectators the personal incentive by which he hopes to thrive—whether
with the head on a stick that he proclaims is Edmund's and
thereby provokes a riot among the English forces (3.3); his convincing Canutus of the policy in the scheme to ingratiate himself
into Edmund's favor (3.5); his success in doing so and the major
victory that follows for Canutus (4.4); or the "nimble wit" in bring-
ing them to single combat in the final act (2.1840). This crass delight in villainy and machination that he shares only with the
spectators throughout the play breaks into the open only once,
in 2.3, when he cackles with pleasure as he observes the physical
mutilation of Turkillus's and Leofric's sons.

While Edricus's interaction with the spectators undoubtedly in-
creases dramatic interest in action that otherwise involves relatively stylized figures, certainly his chief function by his very
presence is to shatter any illusion that the rest of the characters—
namely, Canutus and Edmund—can be entirely free of private
political incentives, whether we are privy to them or not. That is,
although he is the only character to give voice to such concerns,
he—by forcing the spectators to view the various conflicts within
the play through the filter of his ulterior motivations—infuses a
sense of political self-interest that tends to resonate beyond the
individual. The result is a play that, deceptively simplistic on the
surface, contains several political issues to which the Elizabethan
public would be keen to respond and to which government and
church officials would be understandably sensitive.[25] In general,
the political reality of this stage world amounts to nothing less
than a series of power plays in which subjects shuffle between two
leaders for maximum benefit. For their own self-interest, Southampton, Suffolk, and Mercia willingly and openly support the
foreign prince, Canutus, in scene 1, as formerly they supported
his invading father, King Sveyn. Similarly, Turkillus and Leofric's
decision to defect is occasioned not so much by the report that
Edmund's power is sweeping the land as by the fact that they are
out of favor with Canutus. They will not, like Edricus, however,
describe their action in privately selfish terms. Instead, they will
openly claim themselves to be "true noble virtuous gentlemen /
[who] are scorned, disgraced and held in obloquy" (238–39); to
that end, they will return to their "true king" who is "rightly
termed mirror of majesty" (247, 250). The two most powerful
churchmen in the land likewise reflect the political reality of a divided kingdom. Although their confrontation degenerates into

petty name-calling and the bathos of Canterbury's chasing York off the stage while threatening to club him with his crozier staff,[26] they attempt at first to lend dignity to their personal animosities by invoking the labels of "God," "mother country," and "lawful king" (826, 847) to justify their counterposed political positions. Most importantly, the play itself begins and ends with the two kings issuing counterclaims of rightful power. With the plot peppered with indecisive battles (2.3, 2.3, 4.4), church officials fighting among themselves, and the kings dividing up the land after fomenting battles in which countless numbers have been slaughtered, the effect is to strip the concept of kingship bare of legal and spiritual mystification and to focus attention more on the futility of political conflict than on monarchic glory and patriotism.

The playwright, moreover, appears to go out of his way in both the main plot and the parodic digressions to emphasize the manipulation and oppression of the masses. Edmund himself in act 1 speaks of the "captains nowadays [who] / pluck off their soldiers' shoes, nay, sell their lives / to make them rich and gallant to the eye" (3.355–57). Such men, for "private base commodity" (346), hold back payment to the common soldiers and fail to provide food and clothing sufficient for survival. On the Danish side the treatment is even worse; Englishmen during the time of King Sveyn were forced to "honour" their conquerors "as lords / and be [their] slaves, [their] drudges and [their] dogs" (1.116–17); at times, nine out of ten were exterminated through "bloodshed and war, rebellion, sword and fire" (197). Canutus, too, in two instances seems to consider the English commoners little more than bait; his troops prey upon them

> like hungry tigers upon silly kids
> sparing not ancient men for reverence
> nor women for [their] imbecility
> nor guiltless babes for their unspotted life.
>
> (4.1.1349–52)

If that provocative language admittedly comes from Edmund's camp, Canutus himself is indeed a party, in 3.4, to a discussion in which he minimizes military losses by rationalizing that Englishmen have but killed Englishmen, some fighting for Edmund and some for the Danes. In act 5 England is described as a "little isle / whose soil is manured with carcasses / and made a sea with blood of innocents" (2.1897–99). At another point aristocratic disdain for the lower class is cloaked in the sarcastic humor of Edricus's haughty abuses of common decency in the treatment of his parents and the shame he voices on several occasions about his low birth. And the humor points in the same direction when Stitch, a "tool villain" who is a sliver of the old Vice,[27] is forced to exchange garments with his master and thereby suddenly "becomes" the duke of Mercia. The first thing he does is to lace down his erstwhile fellow laborers, now his social inferiors. When one of them fails to address him with both title and respect, he is peremptorily dismissed from the staff, and those remaining are warned to follow "just three foot behind, not above / or beneath" (3.6.1269–70). In such scenes the aping of one's betters, as Talbert observes, parodies the upper class, striking especially at "those derisive persons who pretended to be accomplished in the ways of sixteenth-century gentility."[28]

Despite, then, all the potential high patriotism inherent in this struggle of an early English king against a foreign invader, what emerges in *Edmund Ironside* is a strongly antimonarchic tone. Not only is neither of the contending kings sufficiently powerful to establish peace and social order; both in also falling prey to the flattery and self-serving advice of Edricus fail to harken to wise counsel, and the consequence is mass slaughter of English commoners, for whom the play indicates a general aristocratic disdain and disregard. Moreover, as previously noted, Edmund forgives his archenemy at the moment of military advantage and—seemingly oblivious of the earlier loss of life—accepts him as friend and ally, offering the foreign invader first chocie of the parts of a divided kingdom. Such actions may smack of utopian magnanimity (and certainly, in that sense, it no doubt would provoke a sudden rush of sympathy from the spectator); but, with the spectators not privy to any genuinely compelling motive, the sympathy would be short-lived as they came to realize the sheer stupidity at the level of realpolitik.[29] E. K. Chambers observes that the play "carries no evidence of submission to the Master of the Revels";[30] and both Everitt[31] and Sams[32] have argued that this absence of entry and of references to the play's production is a consequence of its never having been licensed for performance. If that indeed is true, the censor obviously had far more to be concerned with than what they describe as the disrespectful depiction of the archbishop of Canterbury or occasional sacrilegious references by Edricus.

Likenesses to certain works of Shakespeare and Marlowe readily suggest themselves.[33] The scheming villain who delights in his own wit and the success of his machinations and who, through soliloquies and asides, shares a private level of perception with the spectators obviously invites comparison with Barabas or Richard III. Similarly, the conflict of mighty opposites is not unlike the juxtaposition of Mortimer and Edward II or Bolingbroke and Richard II, though, admittedly, the characters of Edmund and Canutus are psychologically far more simplistic. Increasingly sympathetic revelations of suffering in Edward and Richard combine with elements of internalization to provide a sense of character growth more fully explored in Faustus, Brutus, and Hamlet. Canutus and Edmund, to the contrary, are totally flat, neither speaking a private line to the audience and neither seeming to develop in the course of the action. Like Marlowe and Shakespeare, however, the anonymous playwright does gain a degree of character complexity by forcing the spectator to view the two principal figures from sharply contrasting angles.

It is in the combination of the patterns—the internalized villain center stage and the conflict of two powerful protagonists—that the author of *Edmund Ironside* creates a dramatic structure found neither in Marlowe nor in the early Shakespeare, achieving a political perspective that is directly based upon careful control of the spectators' responses. Both Marlowe and Shakespeare gain their focus on the character of the troubled king in the latter stages of the action at the expense of the opposing figure, Marlowe, by intensifying Mortimer's arrant villainy and Isabella's moral degeneracy, Shakespeare, by increasingly depicting Bolingbroke as a political enigma who snaps up opportunities with machinelike precision while refusing to speak of motivation and ambition. The author of *Edmund Ironside,* rather than concentrating on a picture of suffering humanity in either principal, maintains a political focus by holding the two kings emotionally at arm's length even as the action pits them in an endless struggle for supremacy, by providing sporadic glimpses of social oppression and the snobbery of class, and by developing Edricus as a Machiavellian strategist who perpetrates virtually all of the overt villainy in the play and who—in constantly manipulating both men to serve his own devious ends—forces the spectator to become increasingly aware of the shortcomings of the political system that produces them.

The purpose of this study, as noted at the outset, is not to engage the question of Shakespearean authorship, but to examine something of the level of achievement in the play. Inevitably, though, at some point these two concerns do meet. That there is nothing quite like the structure of *Edmund Ironside* in the Shakespeare canon obviously does not mean that he was incapable of creating it, especially in light of his separate use of the two structural patterns found here in combination. On the other hand, it is difficult to imagine Shakespeare's utilizing structural patterns in combination in the late 1580s that he subsequently chose to develop individually, and it is equally difficult to imagine *Ironside*'s psychological simplicity and verbal woodenness from Shakespeare after his achievements in *Richard III* and *Richard II*. If the "semi-Senecan" characteristics identified by Boas[31] correctly place the play in the early 1590s (or, as Sams would have it, in the late 1580s), then the author—despite the end-stopped and monotonous versification, the archaic vocabulary, the use of chorus, dumb show, and messenger, the revenge motive, and the presence of good and evil counselors—possesses structural skills not to be lost on either Marlowe or Shakespeare. If the play dates from 1595 or later, we are dealing with a lesser playwright, but one who in the structure of his work is responsive to the two dominant writers for the stage.

In any event, considered in the context of the developing dramatic form in the last decade of the century, *Edmund Ironside* deserves far better than the two lines accorded by A. H. Bullen in his peremptory verdict that it is "tedious business, sadly wanting in life and movement."[35] Whatever his lack of sophistication in technique and verse, the author not only had more than a rudimentary concept of structure; he also possessed a sense of social criticism that forces us to continue to qualify assumptions that the history play in any general way was a tool of the Tudor political establishment, that it developed solely in response to the tide of patriotism following the Armada,[36] and that it served a firmly didactic purpose[37] in reflecting either a providential view of historical events[38] or a humanist's view of physical action raised to moral spectacle.[39] Though it individually might well have fallen prey to the censor, *Ironside* is evidence that the history play also appealed to the popular audience as an instrument of criticism and agitation, that it used the events of the past to provide for some in the audience a sense of temporary social release.

6

The *Henry VI* Plays

While historical perspective reveals that some eras are more profoundly transitional than others, it is not likely that any age—even our own—can match the impact of the revolution that caught up the minds and spirits of sixteenth-century England. The foundations of modern astronomy are built on the heliocentric concept of the universe, which called into question the centrality of the earth as the center of God's creation. Anatomical studies were beginning to undermine Galenic principles of the body humors fundamental to concepts of medicine and the human personality. Geographical discoveries literally opened new worlds to individuals whose existence had previously been contained within the narrow limits of Europe and its immediate environs. Profound changes were occurring, as well, in the way man reasoned, in his perception of history, in the nature of the family unit and the traditional loyalties inherent to it, in the economic foundations of society, and in institutions of both church and state that had previously provided a degree of stability. In a word, a crisis of authority in virtually every facet of life was to leave few values unchallenged.

Especially the middle years of the century, as Robert Weimann writes, seem to have been "an exceptionally momentous historical period, in which essential assumptions and conditions for the theoretical discourse of the Shakespearean era saw the light of day."[1] The Reformation itself was basically an "act of State,"[2] a crisis of authority creating diverging claims of loyalty or a choice between conflicting authorities—"enough arguments, accusations, scurrility, conviction, abuse and unsettlement to guarantee every possibility of unrest and disturbance in a country always hard to control and impossible to police efficiently."[3] If, as J. J. Scarisbrick has observed, it "concentrated allegiance by reducing the number and diversity of what are today called 'foci of authority,'" it also "broke Heaven and Earth apart by ending communication between Church Militant and Church Triumphant."[4] Joel Hurstfield

71

has noted that a "child born in 1533, the year when Elizabeth was born, . . . if his family was conformist," would have "subscribed to five different versions of the Christian religion by the time that he was twenty-six."[5] Of course, the actual Elizabethan continuum runs from the Jesuits and militant Catholics on the far right to various separatists and fringe sects, like the Family of Love, on the far left.[6]

Meanwhile, a new aristocracy and middle class had emerged, the result of the king's distribution of land and wealth following the dissolution of the monasteries and the vast land enclosures.[7] The subsequent decline in the power and prestige of the older aristocracy allowed Cromwell actively to pursue his concept of state as the sovereign imperial authority, thus pushing the nation toward a higher degree of political unity and central administration. "The horizontal expansion of county government," as Peter Clark writes of the Elizabethan regime, came increasingly in collision with that "vertical growth in power" by which the state "sought to intervene increasingly in the running of local communities, wherever possible absorbing functions previously performed on an informal, seigneurial or neighborly level."[8]

There was a revolution of sorts in communication, as well. With an increased literacy rate and a burgeoning book market, more people were forced to become involved in the discourse of competing religious, political, and intellectual claims. The pamphlet literature of the period indicated a "new sense of citizenship," a "new willingness on the part of the educated, experienced, and potentially articulate citizen to explore the problems of public concern."[9] What is particularly striking about this period when England boiled with new ideas, as Lawrence Stone observes, was the "widespread public participation in significant intellectual debate on every front."[10] The ability to read, said someone at the time, "enableth us better to judge of the doctrines taught" so that "we are better fitted for the combat."[11]

One less enviable consequence of these profound social and political changes was a significant increase in poverty. The social structure was under great stress as a result of the doubling of the population, and economic problems were "brought into sharp relief by the rise in prices which increased by fifty percent in the first forty years of the century and more than doubled in the critical decades from 1540 to 1560."[12] Greed was the leitmotif of the wealthy as England—with increasing numbers of unemployed drifting toward London and the other cities[13]—suffered from "famine, discontent, faction and social dislocation."[14]

The popular theater in Shakespeare's day thrived on this underlying clash of multiple authorities and the general sense of social unrest. "A composite formation in which disparate modes coexisted and intertwined,"[15] it employed fictional strategies to negotiate and legitimate a variety of responses from its socially mixed audiences. While such a dramatic method may well have been the result of the playwrights' humanistic training in the writing of *controversiae*, exercises in which the pupil "would be told to defend each position [in a debate] in turn,"[16] this public entertainment became a profound social force because it addressed issues central to a "society in crisis,"[17] issues to which the spectators brought their own prejudices and predilections and for which they became the "ultimate source of authority in [their] willingness to credit and approve the representation of rule."[18] The public stage was "resonant with long-standing traditions of late-ritual sport and release, game and pastime."[19] Operating between governmental restrictions and courtly sanctions, it developed in the Liberties that Steven Mullaney has described as "ambivalent zones of transition between one realm of authority and another," a "borderland whose legal parameters and privileges were open-ended."[20] In its willingness to explore critically the sources of authority, the stage was a constant source of agitation for the government, which viewed it as a center of potential social unrest.[21] As Stephen Gosson angrily observed: "If the common people which resorte to Theaters bring but an assemblie of Tailers, Tinkers, Cordwayners, Saylers, olde Men, yong Men, Women, Boyes, Girles, and such like, be the iudge of faultes there painted out, the rebuking of manners in that place, is neither lawfull nor conuenient, but to be helde for a kind of libelling, and defaming."[22]

With issues of validation and control so pervasive in the culture, it is surely not accidental that Shakespeare's plays comprise a virtual discourse on authority. The comedies, for example, time and again address the issue of dominance in the marital relationship and the political dimensions of the institution of marriage. *The Taming of the Shrew*, for example, couples blatant competition for supremacy between husband and wife with a daughter who circumvents her father's best-laid plans for a nuptials determined by an attractive dowry and a son who manipulates his father into accepting the financial arrangements of a marriage without benefit of consultation. A similar situation in *The Two Gentlemen of Verona* finds a daughter risking capture by outlaws to reach her banished lover rather than agree to marriage with a suitor sponsored by her father. The struggle between genders is central to *Love's Labor's Lost,* with the relationship between the king of Navarre and the princess of France further complicated by the political issue involving control of Aquitaine. In *A Midsummer Night's Dream* authority is in crisis at every level of the plot. Theseus's romantic relationship with Hippolyta is shadowed by the fact that his fiancée is in Athens only by virtue of his military conquest over her tribe of Amazons; Titania openly flaunts the authority of her male companion and king; Hermia defies both father and political ruler to pursue the desires of her own heart; and Bottom—more comically—refuses to be readily contained by the director of the troupe of thespian handicraftsmen, though certainly he is powerless to oppose Titania's determination to possess him as her lover. The young ladies of Shakespeare's romantic comedy emerge as heroines who heuristically control and teach their mates, thus, in a sense, celebrating female ascendancy when the cult of Elizabeth was at its height; but such experiences ultimately prove to be an act of containment, as marriage—in the inevitable conclusion of the plays—functions to bring the heroine under control through an institution whose very cornerstone, both legally and spiritually, rested on the assumption of male domination. *All's Well That Ends Well,* in fact, strips bare the rhythms and motivations of romantic comedy, exposing with equal force the ferocity of the heroine in her quest to secure a spouse (whether prompted by the desire for self-gratification or by the sacrificial qualities of redemptive love) and the pyrrhic nature of her victory over an individual whose repentance the play not only refuses to confirm but pointedly questions in the final lines. The failure to clarify the nature of Bertram's personality is the source of the play's most powerful ambiguity, since marriage returns to the count of Rossillion whatever authority he had lost as a ward of a king sympathetic to Helena's quest. *Measure For Measure,* performed within months of James's accession to the throne, displays, through the character of Angelo the tyranny of power; but more importantly it foregrounds, in Vincentio, the methods by which power appropriates law and religion to counter challenges to its authority.

The tragedies, likewise, focus on power struggles that define issues central to the age. *Titus Andronicus* opens in a power vacuum in Rome with Saturninus claiming the political inheritance expected by the eldest son of the deceased emperor, in the face of popular factions supporting both his brother, Bassianus, and the Roman general, Titus. After the issue of succession has been resolved, much of the remainder of the action turns on a gender struggle as Tamora, queen of the Goths and wife of Saturninus, maneuvers to gain control of her husband and vengeance against Titus. In one sense, the tragedy of the young lovers in *Romeo and Juliet* is occasioned by Juliet's defiance of parental authority; in another, it results from Prince Escalus's failure to carry out his own edict of death to the next individual who violates the truce between the Capulets and the Montagues; in yet another, the potential for disaster is exacerbated beyond measure by Friar Lawrence's willingness to use the power of his divine office to circumvent legal authority. *Julius Caesar* pits monarchist against republican; but, more significantly, it reflects, in Cassio, the ability of the Machiavellian politician to turn sedition, however motivated, to ulterior purposes that serve private interests. Bullingbrook and Macbeth comprise mirror images of usurpation; Lear and Coriolanus, variations upon the disasters of divided authority. The dramatic focus is not on these bald political issues, to be sure, any more than the primary interest in romantic comedy is on blocking figures rather than nubile youth's first genuine encounter with love. What does seem apparent, however, is that Shakespeare builds into his plots pressure points with which many in his audience could readily identify. Whether or not their engagement is a conscious one, they would possess a cultural and ideological framework that would enhance their interest in a narrative that turns on issues of authority. Their response would obviously be determiend to a large extent by the personal and political biases they bring to the playhouse—in much the same manner that a contemporary spectator's interest in and response to the Broadway production *A Walk in the Woods* or movies like *Kramer Versus Kramer* and *Mississippi Burning* are conditioned by his or her own political or domestic agenda.

Perhaps nowhere is this concept of cultural memory more crucial than in the history plays, in which issues dealing with authority under siege are given a political context that would render them intellectually and emotionally accessible to the spectator of the late 1580s and the 1590s. In this regard, the trilogy of plays on Henry VI, certainly among the earliest of Shakespeare's works, is above all a discourse on the crisis of political discord. In *1 Henry VI* this discord is initiated through an argument that flares between Gloucester and Winchester, is exacerbated by the claims for the crown of the Yorkists and Lancastrians, and is registered most powerfully in the waning of English fortunes in France resulting directly from these internal divisions. Such plays employ what

Jacques Derrida calls the "anterior future,"[23] representing "events at a definable temporal distance from, but along the same line as, the audience's present."[24]

In effect, the opening scenes represent a power struggle between church and state. When the bishop of Winchester praises Henry V for having fought the Lord's battles and claims that the "Church's prayers made him so prosperous" (1.1.32),[25] Gloucester, lord protector during the minority of Henry VI, retorts:

> The Church! where is it? Had not church-men pray'd,
> His thread of life had not so soon decay'd.
> None do you like but an effeminate prince,
> Whom, like a schoolboy, you may overawe.
>
> (33–36)

Words later convert into blows, as Gloucester's "blue coats" attack Winchester's "tawney coats" when the Protector is denied access to the Tower. Accused of being a "manifest conspirator" who contrived to murder the previous king, Winchester counters with claims that Gloucester is "a foe to citizens," a warmonger who overtaxes the people and seeks to overthrow religion in order to "crown himself king and suppress the Prince" (1.3.62, 68). At the Parliament House in 3.1, each accuses the other of treason against the young king even as their followers, deprived of arms, bloody brains and break windows by throwing rocks at their adversaries. By the final act, Winchester, for a "sum of money [he has] promised . . . to his Holiness" (5.5.52–53), has secured a cardinalate. Having "gathered so much treasure, that no man in maner had monie but he," as Holinshed records,[26] he swears that unless Gloucester "stoop[s] and bend[s his] knee" he will "sack this country with a mutiny" (61–62).

If the division between Gloucester and Winchester pivots on the question of how much power the church will exercise in the new reign, the confrontation between Richard Plantagenet and John Beaufort is ultimately far more deadly, interrogating Henry's right to the crown itself. In a scene of his own creation, which Robert Ornstein describes as a "triumph of the dramatic imagination over the inartistic formlessness of Tudor historiography,"[27] Shakespeare sows the seeds of the War of the Roses in the Temple garden. At first the spectator is not even aware of the real point at issue, only that there is a relatively mild disagreement over whether Plantagenet or Somerset has "maintain'd the truth" (2.4.5). After Plantagenet plucks a white rose to symbolize his po-

sition, and Somerset, a red, they agree that the matter will be settled by whoever receives the commitment of the majority of the
lords in the garden. Disagreement soon billows into threat, however, as Somerset vows to "dye [Richard's] rose in a bloody red"
(61), Richard observes that "[t]his quarrel will drink blood another day" (134), and Warwick prophesies

> this brawl to-day,
> Grown to this faction in the Temple Garden,
> Shall send between the Red Rose and the White,
> A thousand souls to death and deadly night.
>
> (124–27)

It becomes clear by the end of the scene that Richard, descended
through his father's marriage from Lionel, duke of Clarence
(third son of Edward III) is claiming royal precedence over Henry
VI, descended from John of Gaunt (the fourth son). The question
depends on whether Richard stands attainted by virtue of the
charges of treason against his father, the earl of Cambridge, and
the following scenes clearly draw the issue of legitimacy into
focus. In 2.5 the lengthy speech of his dying grandfather, Edmund Mortimer, earl of March, further strengthens Plantagenet's
position; old Mortimer describes his own right to the throne following Richard II's death and his imprisonment in the Tower of
London ever since Bullingbrook seized power. And in 3.1 the ban
of attainder is removed when Henry, at the Parliament House,
fully restores Richard "to his blood" as duke of York (158, 171).
With lines now drawn between legal right and ensconced power,
the contention bursts forth anew in Paris between Vernon and
Basset; and, when they go before the king to request trial by combat, the issue is taken up by the principals themselves. Henry's reaction in moderating the dispute is as naïve as his earlier
obliviousness to the danger in elevating Richard to a clear title.
Here the king describes as "slight and frivolous" (4.1.112) that
which will one day cost him his throne and his life. And he
chooses to wear a red rose, incredibly exclaiming that it should
provoke no one to think he inclines to one side more than
another—to Michael Manheim, a mark of his utter failure as a
"politician."[28] From a mere ripple of discontent that gains force
throughout the course of the play, then, Shakespeare depicts an
aristocratic society rent at the very center.

A large part of the action establishes the English army against
the French, and one would suppose that the vast majority of the

Elizabethan audience would unite emotionally against the common enemy. For one thing, the French are arrogant, taunting the English at Orleans as "famish'd . . . ghosts [who] / Faintly besiege us one hour in a month" (1.2.7–8); lacking their "porridge" they look "piteous," "like drowned mice" (9, 12). Talbot, when captured, is displayed in the marketplace as a public spectacle and mocked mercilessly: "Here, said they, is the terror of the French, / The scarecrow that affrights our children so" (1.4.42–43); elsewhere he is ridiculed as "a child, a silly dwarf," a "weak and writhled shrimp" (2.3.22, 23). For another, the French are depicted as faithless. When the duke of Burgundy, in response to Joan of Arc's highly patriotic pleas, agrees to defect to the French and forswear his allegiance to Henry VI, Joan observes wryly in an aside: "Done like a Frenchman—turn and turn again!" (3.3.85). In the English camp his revolt is described as "monstrous treachery" and "false, dissembling guile" (4.1.61, 63); and the disdain assumes a peculiar resonance through juxtaposition with the king's stripping Sir John Falstaff of his knighthood for cowardice in battle and banishing him "on pain of death" (47). As for Joan of Arc, Shakespeare utilizes references to sorcery and a fictionalized confession to relegate her deeds of heroism to the level of devilish machinations.[29] Talbot brands her a witch (1.5.21; 3.2.38) and proclaims that God is the fortress against those who "converse with spirits" (2.1.25). When her fortunes wane, he asserts that "her old familiar is asleep" (3.2.122); and she herself is shown offering her body as "blood-sacrifice" to the fiends of hell: "Where I was wont to feed you with my blood, / I'll lop a member off and give it you" (5.3.20, 14–15). Captured by the English, she forswears her father, calling him a "[d]ecrepit miser" and a "base ignoble wretch" while claiming that she "is descended of a gentler blood" (5.4.7, 8) and that she is a virgin, favored by God, to bring glory to France. Her bold rhetoric collapses, however, when, facing death at the stake, she claims to be with child, first by Alençon, then by Reignier, duke of Anjou.

Despite the anti-French sentiment that such material undoubtedly aroused, the irony is that Shakespeare turns this emotion against the devisive factions in England. Ultimately, of course, France during the reign of Henry VI was for the English a dusty road to death and defeat. Holinshed is brutally frank: "And whie? Euen because the deuilish diuision that reigned in England, so incombred the heads of the noble men there, that the honor of the realme was cleerlie forgotten, so that (to conclude) the daie appointed came, but succour looked for came not" (3:228). Similarly, the play—through the voice of a messenger—leaves no doubt where the blame for this destruction lies:[30]

> No treachery, but want of men and money.
> Amongst the soldiers this is muttered,
> That here you maintain several factions;
> And whilst a field should be dispatch'd and fought,
> You are disputing of your generals.
> One would have ling'ring wars with little cost;
> Another would fly swift, but wanteth wings;
> A third thinks, without expense at all,
> By guileful fair words peace may be obtain'd.
>
> (1.1.69–77)

Later, it is specifically the "vulture of sedition / Feed[ing] in the bosom" (4.3.47–48) of York and Somerset that costs England her glory and Talbot his life. York claims that he is unable to send reinforcements to the army because Somerset withholds the squadrons of cavalry (4.3.25), while Somerset maintains that York has "[t]oo rashly" set the army on "this unheedful, desperate, wild adventure" (4.4.3, 7). As Talbot dies with his dead son in his arms, the spectators' anger is focused primarily on the "fraud of England, not the force of France" (36). Even the breach in the uneasy truce with which part 2 concludes is attributed directly to self-serving scheming on the part of the English. Alençon may observe privately that the dauphin will break the compact "when [his] pleasure serves" (5.4.164), but it is the English who do so. The "goodly peace" intended to "stop effusion of our Christian blood / And stablish quietness on every side" (5.1.5, 9–10) is doomed to failure by Suffolk's lust. Whereas the arrangement calls for Henry to take as his queen the daughter of the earl of Armagnac, "near knit" to the French king, to "surer bind this knot of amity" (16), Suffolk schemes to serve his personal ambitions by convincing the young and impressionable English ruler to set that contract aside in favor of Margaret of Anjou. Through such a union Suffolk vows to rule "her, the King, and realm" (5.5.108). Holinshed not only blames the loss of Aquitaine on this foolish marriage and Armagnac's subsequent enmity, but also the ultimate collapse of the Lancastrian rule: "But most of all it should seeme, that God was displeased with this marriage: for after the confirmation thereof, the kings freends fell from him, both in England and in France, the lords of his realm fell at diuision, and the commons rebelled in such sort, that finallie after manie fields foughten, and manie thousands of men slaine, the king at length was deposed, and his sonne killed, and this queene sent home againe, with as much miserie and sorrow as she was receiued with pompe and triumph" (3:208).

Part 1 concludes, then, without resolution of the several power struggles that tear England from within. The playwright, moreover, intensifies the political factionalism by subtly revealing the class division inherent in such a feudal society. And it is hardly likely that commoners in the audience would miss allusions that would sharpen their disdain for an aristocracy not only divided and destructive but also arrogant and supercilious. The pattern is simply too pervasive to be accidental—Gloucester's fury at being challenged at the Tower by "dunghill grooms" (1.3.14); Somerset's branding Plantagenet a "yeoman" (2.4.81), and Warwick's taking exception to one of Plantagenet's birth being called a "crestless yeoman" (85); Talbot's sneer that the French, who refuse to leave the battlements of Rouen and fight in the open field, are like "[b]ase muleters" and "peasant footboys" (3.2.68, 69); Gloucester's charge that Sir John Falstaff's cowardice would disgrace even a "common man" (4.1.31), and Talbot's pledge that Falstaff will be "quite degraded, like a hedge-born swain" (43); Talbot's son's fear that, should he leave the battlefield in order to save himself, he would be compared to "peasant boys" (4.6.48); Suffolk's preposterous remark, while attempting to convince King Henry to disregard his betrothal with the earl of Armagnac's daughter, that only "worthless peasants bargain for their wives" (5.5.53). Obviously the nobles must constantly confirm their assumptions of superiority through expressions of contempt for those beneath them; their deeds, to the contrary, prove that such social status is only the accident of birth, wealth, and the power it confers. Indeed, the most insidious consequence of their animosities is that the livelihood of commoners who want no part in it—English and French alike—have been affected. A French sentinel, ordered to stand night guard at Orleans, remarks: "Thus are poor servitors, / When other sleep upon their quiet beds, / Constrain'd to watch in darkness, rain, and cold" (2.1.5–7). And, concerning the factionalism between Gloucester and Winchester, Holinshed records: "Sure it is that the whole realme was troubled with them and their partakers: so that the citizens of London were faine to keep dailie and nightlie watches, and to shut vp their shops for fear of that which was doubted to have issued of their assembling of people about them" (3:146). That the common folk seem to be less contentious by nature than the fractious noblemen is suggested in the wry comment of the mayor of London as he attempts to quell their disturbance: "I myself fight not once in forty year" (1.3.91).

Commoners play a larger and far more complex role in *2 Henry VI*. To be sure, they continue to serve as objects of aristocratic insult. They are "base cullions" to Margaret (1.3.40), "rude unpolish'd hinds" to Suffolk (3.2.271); one is a "[b]ase dunghill villain and mechanical" to York (1.3.193); the duchess of Gloucester is contemptuously described as a "base-born callet" (1.3.83), Warwick, as an "untutor'd churl" (3.2.213). Beyond that, however, they provide a clearer reflection of the oppressiveness of a class-based society. A petitioner before the palace in 1.3, for example, claims that Winchester's agent has seized his house, lands, wife, and all; another, that Suffolk has unlawfully enclosed the commons of Melford for his own use (1.3). When Saunder Simpcox is exposed for fraudulently asserting that he has been miraculously cured of his blindness, his wife pleads "we did it for pure need" (2.1.154). At other moments they reveal how dangerous and how destructive such an oppressed class can be when pushed too far. Commoners threaten violence in 3.2 unless Suffolk be immediately executed or banished; and in 4.1, in a scene foregrounding the utter meaningless of title and status when individuals are removed from the social setting that physically enforces them, the citizens make good their threats, beheading him at sea.[31] In such a setting Suffolk's "Look on my George, I am a gentleman" (4.1.29) is incredibly pompous, and his branding the commoners "jaded groom" (52), "[b]ase slave" (67), "paltry, servile, abject drudges" (105), "vulgar groom" (128), and "vild besonians" (134) simply assures his death. Suffolk, in a word, is so obsessed with social standing that he is incapable of civil conversation with common citizens. Shakespeare obviously adds this dialogue to emphasize the aristocratic arrogance. Holinshed reports only that "the capteine of that barke with small fight entered into the dukes ship, and perceiuing his person present, brought him to Douer road, and there on the one side of a cocke boat caused his head to be strucken off, and left his bodie with the head lieing there on the sands" (3:220).

Jack Cade's activities grimly reveal a society that has virtually collapsed from within. His macabre execution of a clerk for knowing how to read and write is exceeded only by his desire to kill "[a]ll scholars, lawyers, courtiers, gentlemen" (4.4.36) and his beheading of Lord Say for erecting a grammar school and thereby having "most traitorously corrupted the youth of the realm"

(4.7.32–33). He intends to burn London Bridge, the Tower, and all records of the kingdom. There is no denying that such anarchic horrors reflect the unraveling of the basic foundations of civilized society—"moral and social anarchy" invalidating through travesty the normal ties of kinship[32]—but it is equally clear that his rebellion is directly prompted by crass irresponsibility on the part of the aristocracy.[33] Most significantly, York cunningly manipulates the action to serve his own political ends, encouraging Cade's delusion that he is descended from the Mortimers and thus is the rightful heir to the throne. Whether Cade succeeds or fails is of little concern to him, since he plans with his army to "reap the harvest which that rascal sow'd" (3.1.381).

Moreover, Cade's widespread destruction is possible only because of a total power vacuum in the English government, a moment when the nexus of competing self-interests that normally drive society become mutually destructive.[34] The enmity between Gloucester and the cardinal, central to the action of part 1, flares anew; and Somerset, Buckingham, Suffolk, and Queen Margaret also grow envious of the lord protector's power. York stands aside, smugly biding his time as his enemies at court begin to self-destruct.[35] When arrested on trumped-up charges of high treason, Humphrey lashes out at those who plot against his life as the "prologue" to their individual devious designs:[36]

> Beaufort's red sprakling eyes blab his heart's malice,
> And Suffolk's cloudy brow his stormy hate;
> Sharp Buckingham unburthens with his tongue
> The envious load that lies upon his heart;
> And dogged York, that reaches at the moon,
> Whose overweening arm I have pluck'd back,
> By false accuse doth level at my life.
> And you, my sovereign lady, with the rest,
> Causeless have laid disgraces on my head,
> And with your best endeavor have stirr'd up
> My liefest liege to be mine enemy.
>
> (3.1.154–64)

The level of conflict is so intense throughout the play that on two occasions the nobles descend to the most elemental physical level, leaving the stage in high dudgeon to fight it out personally off stage; Gloucester and Beaufort in 2.1, Warwick and Suffolk in 3.2.

York, as it turns out, has read the political situation correctly, and he is the prime benefactor of the events following Gloucester's death. Charged with the murder, Suffolk is banished from the land, and the cardinal, in the throes of a fatal apoplexy, acknowledges his role in the assassination. The queen's aspirations are blunted by separation from her lover and partner in ambition, and Warwick and Salisbury confirm their support for the Yorkist claim. Henry, gravely weakened by the dissension that has gnawed his kingdom from within, is now prey to external forces—the temporarily successful rebellion of Cade and his band of commoners that reaches from Kent into the streets of London, followed by the far more formidable forces of Richard, who soundly defeats the royal army at Saint Albans and, in the final lines of the play, triumphantly speaks of pursuing the king to London to achieve ultimate military victory.

The factionalism in part 1, in effect, has hardened into political anarchy in part 2, and the earlier struggles to maintain English holdings in France are virtually forgotten. Somerset's report to Henry that "all your interest in those territories / Is utterly bereft you: all is lost" (3.1.84–85) evokes hardly a response. The absence of authority at the political center clearly has rendered England her own worst enemy. At the heart of this political impotence is the king himself, respected by neither snarling nobles nor rebellious commoners.[37] Those in the court repeatedly observe his deficiencies as a leader. He lacks courage, according to Queen Margaret; his mind is so "bent to holiness" that she would have the pope "carry him to Rome" (1.3.55, 62). And later in the military struggle with Richard, she overtly challenges his "manhood, wisdom, and defense" (5.2.75). Gloucester describes him as a king who stands on legs not firm enough "to bear his body" (3.1.190); and Richard, claiming to be "[m]ore like a king, more kingly in my thoughts" (5.1.29), would have him "obey that knows not how to rule" (6):

> No; thou art not King;
> Not fit to govern and rule multitudes,
>
> . . . .
> That head of thine doth not become a crown:
> Thy hand is made to grasp a palmer's staff
> And not to grace an aweful princely scepter.
> . . . .
> And with the same to act controlling laws.
>
> (93–94, 96–98, 103)

Time and again Henry capitulates under duress, whether in allowing Gloucester to be arrested although he knows his uncle to be guiltless, or in agreeing to banish Suffolk in the face of commoners' demands, or in deceitfully attempting to hide Somerset after informing Richard that he is under arrest. His image in the commoners' eyes is hardly better; Cade observes that in Henry's reign their plight is to "live in slavery to the nobility," to break their backs with burdens, to lose the shelter over their heads, and to see their wives and daughters ravished before their eyes (4.8.28–32). Henry's own desire to escape the responsibilities of leadership best describes the political ineptitude that wreaks destruction upon the land: "Was ever king that joy'd an earthly throne / And could command no more content than I? . . . Was never subject long'd to be a king / As I do long and wish to be a subject" (4.9.1–2, 5–6).

In *3 Henry VI*, Henry fades into little more than a figurehead, at one point agreeing to disinherit his children, at another abdicating power in favor of a double protectorate. Certainly he continues to draw invective from friend and foe alike. Escaping from York in the opening scene by stealing away from his own forces during battle, he is labeled "fearful" (25), "bashful" (41), "wretched" (216), and "timorous" (231). When he agrees that York shall reign after his death, he is told that he lacks the courage of his father (63) and that he "preferrest [his] life before [his] honor" (246). Later, Clifford charges that, "hadst [he] sway'd as kings should do" (2.6.14), York would never have made headway. Clearly Henry grows to detest the political process, preferring to bequeath the throne to Richard rather than provoke a fight in the Parliament House (1.1.195–200) and thus to leave his own son only his "virtuous deeds" (2.2.49). He later reacts with disgust to the sight of his adversary's head on a pole in York and would willingly exchange his lot for that of a "homely swain" (2.5.22). When restored to the throne, he promptly delegates his power to others (4.6.41); and his comments in the face of death provoke only a prayer of forgiveness for himself and for his murderer (5.6.60).

With the active role of the king for all intents and purposes eliminated in part 3, the crisis of authority reaches its gravest depths as the various factions of the earlier plays coalesce into the internecine struggle between Yorkists and Lancastrians and the action of the play degenerates into a continuous series of battles. To achieve this focus on what amounts to nothing less than national political suicide, Shakespeare, more specifically, organizes his material around seven battles, with each claiming a savage toll on aristocracy and commoner alike.[38] Of one battle alone, for example, Holinshed reports that "in these two daies were slaine (as they that knew it wrote) on both parts six and thirtie thousand seuen hundred threescore & sixteen persons, all English and of one nation" (3:278). Queen Margaret emerges as the driving force as the Lancastrians successfully attack at Wakefield (1.2) and again at Saint Albans (2.1).[39] At Towton fortunes are reversed in a furious struggle (2.3) that culminates in Henry's escape into Scotland and Edward's coronation in London (2.6). The wheel reverses once more when Edward is captured at Warwick (4.3) and Henry receives the crown anew (4.6); but Edward, in turn, seizes Henry in London and is again proclaimed king (4.8). At Barnet (5.2) and at Tewkesbury (5.4), Edward is again victorious, securing for his brief lifetime what he vainly boasts will be York's "lasting joy" (5.7.46).

Shakespeare emphasizes the darker side of civilization not only through the endless series of battles that drone throughout the play but also through the primitive level of ferocity in man's treatment of his fellow man. There is a kind of hideous delight in Clifford's stabbing of young Rutland and of his taunting the father by holding up a handkerchief stained with the lad's blood. Richard himself is forced to sit on a molehill; and when a paper crown is placed upon his head, Margaret mocks him mercilessly: "Stamp, rave, and fret, that I may sing and dance" (1.4.91). Later, when Clifford is killed by Richard's sons, they become infuriated that his death occurs before he receives the full measure of their mockery. They exercise their full scorn upon Henry's son, Ned, however, as in his mother's sight they taunt the youth and stab him repeatedly. As for Margaret herself, they refuse her the "ease" of death, preferring that she live to experience unceasing horror. When Henry is subsequently stabbed to death in the Tower, Richard, duke of Gloucester, delights in first describing the agonizing death of the young prince, and he cuts the king off midsentence when the distraught father attempts a verbal retort.[40] Clearly the murders throughout the play move beyond political execution or battlefield casualty to a level of bestial savagery rendered all the more grotesque by the fact that the human mind, at such a level of brutality, can sense a perverse pleasure in the deed.

This regressive behavior is further intensified by the general lack of fealty in a society stripped of all values save those of power and survival. At the outset, Richard extracts from Henry a pledge that the crown will pass to the Yorks after the king's death. In the context of this political anarchy, however, "an oath is of no moment" (1.2.22), hardly worth the breath requried to utter it; both sides immediatley lay plans to violate it.[41] Later, when King Edward declares "[m]y will shall stand for law" (4.1.50), he has reduced his office, the badge of lawful society, to little more than a caricature of the mob leader, Cade, who in part 2 exclaimed that his mouth would be parliament (4.7.14–15). From his forswearing of his betrothal to Lady Bono in order to satisfy his own lust, to Warwick's renunciation of fidelity to Edward as he joins the Lancastrian faction, the play is shot through with broken vows. King Lewis of France, in pledging that articles of peace shall be drawn between England and France, violates an earlier promise to lend suport to Queen Margaret; within moments, Lewis turns again, vowing to aid Edward's enemies in their struggle to depose him. A similar double violation is seen in Clarence, who at one moment deserts his brother Edward to marry Warwick's daughter and thus align himself with the Lancastrians, then at another proves renegade once more when Edward's political fortunes rise:

> proud-hearted Warwick, I defy thee,
> And to my brother turn my blushing cheeks.
> Pardon me, Edward, I will make amends.
>
> (5.1.98–100)

All too obviously, one's word is good in this society only so long as it serves self-interests.

The scene that best captures the price that one must pay for humanity run wild is Shakespeare's own, a highly charged moment in which the crisis of authority that has been at the heart of all three plays reaches a powerful climax. Obviously, in a society that has lost all moorings of both law and loyalty, only the family unit remains as a final bastion of love, support, and mutality; and here even this final value is destroyed as Henry—the living symbol of failed law—must observe a father holding a son he has killed on one side of the stage, and a son, a father he has killed on the other.[42] All of the king's references to God's will ring hollow indeed in the face of the son's lament: "Who's this? O God! it is my father's face, / Whom in this conflict I, unawares, have kill'd him" (2.5.61–62). And Henry's allusions to the desirability of the simple shepherd's life seem beyond criminal in their irresponsibility in the face of the father's anguish:

Ah, no, no, no, it is mine only son!
. . . .
O pity, God, this miserable age!
What strategems! how fell! how butcherly!
Erroneous, mutinous, and unnatural,
This deadly quarrel daily doth beget!

(83, 88–91)

It is only fitting that the closure of part 3 is open-ended. A society so bereft of values is hardly likely to find renewal in a ruler like Edward, whose power rests on brutal suppression, murder, and lust. As the scene concludes, the Machiavellian Richard stands in the wings, biding the opportunity to seize power as he gives a Judas kiss to his brother and cries "All hail!" when he means "all harm!" (5.7.34). If, contrary to Jan Kott's claim, there are gods in Shakespeare,[43] they have been appropriated in the *Henry VI* plays by humans caught up in a society of divided authorities and competing ideologies with whom Shakespeare's auditors would share an uncomfortable affinity.

Whether in the theater or the study, *King John* has always evoked a baffling variety of responses. Spectators frequently do not quite know what to make of an English king who bravely defies the pope in one scene only to capitulate abjectly in the next and who dies in slow agony on stage without the slightest touch of retrospection—or of an ambitious young bastard of Richard I whose proclamations of self-serving commodity convert to a somewhat brassy display of patriotism—or of a dauphin who, moments after adamantly refusing the church's order to cease aggression against John, peremptorily withdraws his forces from English soil at the point of highest military advantage. Critics in various ways have long suggested that something significant is at work in Shakespeare's developing concept of drama. The present essay argues that the closure of *King John* is a key to Shakespeare's larger pattern, a design by which, in effect, he shapes from the chronicle play a form that—free from Tudor ideology—reveals historical process as human process determined innately by fundamental self-interest, a concept vital to the nature of his subsequent histories and tragedies.

In this play of "profound moral complexities,"[1] one of the most curious lines occurs in act 4 in John's order to the Bastard to seek out his rebellious lords and request that they return to him: "I have a way to win their loves again. / Bring them before me" (4.2.168–69).[2] Pembroke, Salisbury, Bigot, and other English lords, believing young Arthur to be a victim of John's foul play, have threatened disobedience to the tyrant: "This must not be thus borne. This will break out / To all our sorrows, and ere long I doubt" (101–2). A scene later, they will secretly agree to meet with Cardinal Pandulph in order to work out the details of their defection to France; Salisbury even notes that he has a private message from Lewis, the dauphin, imputing much love and honor to the English nobles. Moments later, their discovery of Arthur's broken body seems to provide a convenient justification for the direct and flagrant rebellion they, in fact, have already determined:

> The King hat dispossess'd himself of us.
> We will not line his thin bestained cloak
> With our pure honors, nor attend the foot
> That leaves the print of blood where e'er it walks.
>
> (4.3.23–26)

Their response to the Bastard's message that John commands their return is to repudiate their loyalty to the king and, kneeling before Arthur's body, to pledge themselves to "the worship of revenge" (72).

John knows his situation is critical, and his using the Bastard as an emissary to the lords is clearly an act by which he hopes to contain their insurrection. The question, quite simply, concerns what John plans to tell them; what is the "way" in which he hopes "to win their love again"? Perhaps he has already decided to capitulate to Pandulph (something he does with no forewarning in act 5, scene 1), and he assumes such a peacemaking effort and his implicit repentance will regain their support. Perhaps, as H. H. Furness, Jr., suggests, he has decided to blame Authur's death entirely on Hubert,[3] something he does indeed attempt to do a few lines later with feigned indignation clothed in hypocritical piety. Perhaps he assumes that the presence of a foreign invader will fire his lords with a patriotism that will mitigate their rebellious fury; this is a possibility, since a messenger has brought him news only moments earlier of his mother's death in France and of the landing of a mighty French force on English soil, and since immediately after his command he speaks of wanting "no subject enemies / When adverse foreigners affright [his] towns" (4.2.171–72).[4] Perhaps, since Faulconbridge has just reported a general discontent among the commoners, who are "strangely fantasied, / Possess'd with rumors, full of idle dreams" (144–45), John assumes that aristocratic self-interest will dictate their renewed support in order to prevent a general rebellion among the masses.[5] Perhaps C. Porter is correct in assuming that John has decided to make concessions inherent to the Magna Charta,[6] an issue that Shakespeare does not otherwise mention in the play. Certainly the one thing he cannot intend is to claim that Arthur is still alive, since at that particular moment he believes the young prince to have been murdered by Hubert on royal command.

While one assumption may be more plausible than others, the

drama does not admit a definitive answer. Admittedly, a spectator without benefit of retrospective contemplation would experience nothing of such a variety of responses, but, by the same token, any one or two explanations might well occur to any given spectator. The salient point is that, whatever John might have in mind by the comment, it does not work. If he plans to announce his capitulation to Pandulph, for instance, we know that intention wins him only the disdain of the Bastard:

> O inglorious league!
> Shall we, upon the footing of our land,
> Send fair-play orders and compremise,
> Insinuation, parley, and base truce
> To arms invasive?
>
> (5.1.669)

and the defiance of the dauphin and his English defectors:

> I will not return
> Till my attempt be so much glorified
> As to my ample hope was promised.
>
> (5.2.110–12)

If John's plan is to blame Arthur's death on Hubert, we see that intention exploded into a series of almost pathetically comic contradictions. Hubert responds to John's accusation with an admission that Arthur still lives, in turn becomes another emissary to the lords with that news, ironically arrives when Arthur lies dead before them, and—even though we know him to be the only individual in the stage world to have acted on grounds of selfless mercy in sparing Arthur's eyesight—is blamed for the murder and threatened with death.

Any presumption that John harbors of rallying his lords to patriotic fervor at the report of a French invasion is again dashed with high irony. Whereas in *The Troublesome Reign of John King of England* the English lords defect only after seeing Arthur's body, and in Holinshed's *Chronicles* only—thirteen years following Arthur's death—when they are demanding that John consent to the liberties granted in the Magna Charta and the Charta de Foresta, Shakespeare depicts their defection as occurring before the Bastard even reaches them, well before they know Arthur in fact to be dead. Their concern, clearly, is not a sense of patriotism or a lack of it but their "safety" and "the Dolphin's love," which they have been promised (4.3.12, 16).

Whatever John means by the line, the larger question is what Shakespeare meant by it. Obviously the choice of using it is his own; it is in neither *The Troublesome Reign* nor Holinshed. Possibly the command is purely a dramaturgic device by which to heighten the tension of the scene. After all, John has no more than sent the Bastard on his way to the nobles when Hubert arrives and, with his news that Arthur lives, is dispatched as yet another messenger. With the lords' discovering Arthur's body between the arrival of the two, what is admittedly a flurry of events is rendered coherent and dramatically effective. Also, as William Matchett has noted, this particular sequence provides a crucial test for the Bastard, who must choose between the lords' and Hubert's conflicting claims concerning responsibility for Arthur's death and between loyalty to John or to the rebels with their emotional pledge of vengeance.[7] Yet another possibility, Shakespeare may have intended John's assertion that he has a way to regain his subjects' loyalty as nothing more than an act of rattled desperation, a signal of the king's loss of political control and of his need to buy time by whatever means comes to mind.

Most likely, Shakespeare's real reason is—whatever the individual spectator's assumption—to raise an anticipation only to dash it; in the failure of each of these possibilities lies the convolution of ironies and ambiguities with which the play concludes.[8] John's comment, in a word, seems to set in motion a series of actions that methodically cancel out any presumed moral or political virtues in the historical process, reducing the government and society to the chaos of individual machination, at worst, and an unstable nexus of conflicting self-interests, at best; the deity "is spoken for by voices which not only contradict each other but repeatedly belie themselves."[9] Lewis, leader of the French forces, for example, warmly welcomes the English nobles, receiving them in a highly ritualistic manner as he draws up a contractual agreement, and then takes the sacrament in a pledge of keeping his faith "firm and inviolable" (5.2.7). No doubt without realizing the irony, he mocks any high principle that might have motivated their joining him by assuring them they shall "thrust [their] hand as deep / Into the purse of rich prosperity / As Lewis himself" (60–62). Similarly, any assumption that he is fighting as champion of the holy church against the heretical English king collapses when he refuses Pandulph's command to "wind up" the "threat-'ning colors" of war now that John is reconciled with Rome (73):

What is that peace to me?
I . . . claim this land for mine,
And now it is half conquer'd, must I back
Because that John hath made his peace with Rome?
Am I Rome's slave?

(92–93, 94–97)

Lewis's final act of treachery is prevented only by the dying Count Melun's revelation to the English lords that they "are bought and sold! . . . He means to recompense the pains you take / By cutting off your heads" (5.4.10, 15–16).

The defecting English lords hardly fare better. Their display of patriotic affection—lamenting that "we, the sons and children of this isle" must take such action to cure "the infection of the time" (5.2.25, 20)—brings tears to Lewis's eyes. As noted, however, their patriotism seems little more than self-interest when Lewis promises them material compensation. And when the dauphin, in their presence and without a single protest, defies Pandulph, they suddenly find themselves fighting against both their country and their religion. It is surely difficult for the spectator to suppress at least a degree of repulsion in their sudden desire, purely in order to save their lives, to "untread" their "damned flight," to "Stoop low," to "run on in obedience / Even to our ocean, to our great King John" (5.4.52, 55, 56–57). When—"their lilies thrice-gilded"[10]—they drag in young Henry as their advocate, it is not, considering the full context, a particularly auspicious entrance for England's future king. As Virginia Mason Vaughan has recently observed, the "English nobles return to the fold not because they are true but because they discover that Lewis is untrue."[11]

Certainly the final phase of John's reign is so pathetic as to derail any tendency to side with the king on grounds of fundamental nationalism. Admittedly, throughout the play Shakespeare has forced us to view John from a variety of perspectives, provoking both sympathy and disdain;[12] as Michael Manheim has observed, in comparison with his role in *The Troublesome Reign,* John "seems more genuinely heroic in facing down the Cardinal and blacker than ever in his relations with Prince Arthur."[13] But, in any case, his capitulation to Rome, in the face of his earlier vaunted assertions of English independence, strikes the spectator as nothing less than treason, a desperate effort to save his life and his kingship. That these are his final moments of physical health might well also be symbolically ironic. The Bastard, in his subsequent confrontation with the dauphin, describes John as "well pre-par'd," as smiling at his "pigmy" opponents (5.2.134, 135); the "gallant monarch is in arms" and hovers "like an eagle" (148, 149); in "warlike" John's "forehead sits / A bare-ribb'd death" (176–77). In actuality, we see John, six lines later, sick at heart and wasted by fever (5.3.3–4), and our next view (scene 7) finds him in agonized death throes. Moreover, the last moments evince from John not a hint of remorse or spiritual sensitivity. There is simply no evidence to support Ribner's claim that John is sincerely repentant for his sins, and only slightly more credible is Adrien Bonjour's observation that the final words of Prince Henry and the Bastard are "like a pardon giving lasting rest to a tormented soul."[14] Whatever the degree of sympathy from the spectator, it is provoked entirely by the spectacle of the suffering man.

Then, too, the Roman church offers no haven for the spectator who, in his search for some abiding principle or value, becomes increasingly dislocated during the play's closure. John's poisoning by a monk is but the final treacherous deed of a church that throughout has consistently acted not on spiritual but on tem-poral principle. One has only to consider the behavior of Cardinal Pandulph to find specific examples. Whether in his excommuni-cating John for his failure to recognize the Roman candidate for archbishop of Canterbury, followed by his subsequent abolition of the papal curse when the king agrees to become a vassal of the church; in his inciting the French to war on the infidel John so as to bring him to heel, followed by the later command that Lewis peremptorily cease his aggression and retire from England; or in his counseling Lewis to invade England even though he knows that event will surely cost young Arthur his life, the cardinal is a major source of England's problems, his function "nothing less than the conjuring of chaos in the achieving of Rome's goals."[15] Shakespeare has indeed toned down the violent anti-Catholic sen-timent of *The Troublesome Reign,* but what remains is an all-the-more insidious pattern of religion pandering to power politics. It is thematically appropriate that an arm of the church is surrepti-tiously present in the events leading to John's unnatural death.

Many critics seize upon Faulconbridge as the positive force, whether humanistic or political, in the play's final scenes. Presum-ably borrowed from *The Troublesome Reign,* the Bastard becomes in Shakespeare's hand, in the early acts, a more cynical observer of a commodity-driven world; then, according to prevailing views, he experiences a kind of maturation through which he is pre-pared to speak for the body politic in the face of foreign invaders and of only recently quelled outbreaks of civil dissension. Matchett, for example, sees him as changing from a "naive enthusiast [who] follow[s] chance to a man of mature insight and ability,"[16] and James L. Calderwood sees a full maturation in his withstanding the temptation to usurp Henry's right in the final moments.[17] We should be permitted to wonder, though, if we have not chosen a hero by default. He may indeed appear to be more worthy of sympathy than any of the surrounding figures, but, as Blanpied notes, "What we hear beneath the highly polished rhetoric . . . is a persistent grating lust for violence and blood."[18] When, following his denunciation of John's deference to Rome, he is given control of the English forces, he leads John's army to, at best, a standoff with Lewis. Hubert reports to John in act 5, scene 3, that things go "badly" for the English forces, and the king in scene 7 dies on the Bastard's own report that successful defense against the approaching Lewis is virtually impossible. Lewis himself, in scene 5 boasts that the French are lords of the battlefield and that the English have "measure[d] backward their own ground / In faint retire" (3–4); he eagerly awaits the "fair adventure" (22) of the next day's battle. The Bastard's patriotic oratory, in other words, does not translate into deeds, and clearly he is the most surprised figure on stage to learn in the final scene of the dauphin's decision to return to France, leaving to Pandulph the arrangement of a negotiated peace. In a word, Pandulph—not he—is responsible for whatever peace comes to England. He obviously can claim no responsibility for the storm that destroys a large part of Lewis's reinforcements; and he, having suffered a similar loss of troops, must watch the struggle wind down with a sense of futility on both sides.

The Bastard puts the best face on this turn of events, to be sure; and the play ends on his rousing assertion that England shall never fall so long as Englishmen are true to one another, words almost universally praised as effecting a closure that points toward the resurgence of a powerful and unified kingdom. Such a reading is undercut, however, by what A. R. Braunmuller, in his recent Oxford edition of the play, claims to be the proverbial nature of these final words, as having a quality of cliché that at least some spectators would perceive as ironically appropriate to Shakespeare's shaping (or unshaping) of this history play. Eugene Waith may well speak of the Bastard's "unexpectedly total commitment to the cause of his country" as a "*coup de theatre*";[19] but, as David Kastan correctly observes, Faulconbridge's "vision of England 'true' to itself is no less a fiction than his vision of

England's dauntless king," even as John lies dying.[20] Moreover, when one considers that Shakespeare's history of Henry IV is soon to depict the ravages of civil war at a later point in time, the words become almost as ominously prophetic as those final lines of *Henry V*, in which the chorus points to Henry VI and his bleeding England. In both cases the cold chill of reality tempers the fire of political patriotism.

Strikingly different is the more traditional closure of *The Troublesome Reign*. There the focus throughout is more directly on the title figure, and the treatment far more sympathetic. The prologue announces the story of a "warlike Christian" Englishman who endured peril and pain "For Christ's true faith" (5–6),[21] and, true to character, John describes his ultimate submission to Cardinal Pandulph as only an act of dissembling (*2 TR*, 283). Praised even by Arthur for his stamina and mettle (*1 TR*, 451), he nonetheless possesses a modesty and sensitivity not present in Shakespeare, a quality evident in his initial comments that he is unworthy of so high a place as the kingship (*1 TR*, 10). He is also a man capable of moral introspection bordering on anagnorisis in his dying moments:

> The world hath wearied me, and I have wearied it.
> . . . .
> Me thinks I see a cattalogue of sinne,
> Wrote by a friend in Marble characters,
> The least enough to loose my part in heaven.
>
> . . . .
> Dishonor did attaynt me in my life,
> And shame attendeth *John* unto his death.
> (*2 TR*, 798, 1046–48, 1066–67)

In *The Troublesome Reign,* more specifically, additional emphasis on the villainy of the Roman church, on John's penitence in the final lines, of Henry's firm assumption of kingship, and on the impact of the reunited English state once Lewis has decided to abort his invasion and return to France—all serve to provoke a sense of coherence, unity, and patriotism traditionally associated with the English history play. It is interesting to note, as well, that the major points comprising the closure of *The Troublesome Reign* are also found in Holinshed. There, too, collusion described at some length between two members of the abbey or between a convert and John's servants brings about the king's death. In both there is specific reference to John's concern with religion, Holinshed noting that the deeds of this "noble & righteous prince"[22] reflect a zeal to religion, and *The Troublesome Reign* depicting his conviction that his agony is inflicted upon him for his "grievous sins" and his fear that God is not sufficiently merciful to forgive his evil deeds. In both, young Henry assumes the kingship in a demonstrably impressive manner. Holinshed reports that the defecting nobles were prompted to return by the great potential they saw in Henry and that they, "with one consent, proclaimed the yoong gentleman king of England" (4:48); and in *The Troublesome Reign* Henry confidently and successfully challenges Lewis and a continued French presence in England.

Shakespeare's *King John*, to the contrary, lacks such generically comforting touches. His aim is to present the character in starker and more ambiguous detail, with equally persuasive views of the usurper, the world-be murderer, the terror-stricken capitulator, the sufferer, the patriot, and the kingly defender of his nation against the avarice of France and the superstition of Rome. For the same reason Shakespeare apparently rejects those scenes in which anti-Catholic sentiment is so flagrantly exploited that sympathy would automatically accrue to John—for instance, the scene of venery between Friar Lawrence and Nun Alice and the scene in which a monk proclaims without remorse that he has committed a righteous murder against a king who dared to challenge the true church. John's poisoning, described in only five lines of the text, is the act of a single fanatical monk. Similarly, Shakespeare depicts Arthur as simple and innocent, deleting all traces of an impetuosity, which helps to explain and to meliorate, if not to justify, John's villainy. Neither is there a single word of remorse on John's lips through the entire ordeal. Absent, too, is any significant degree of confidence in the young Henry, either of word or deed. The nobles swear their loyalty, and Salisbury even observes that Henry will "set a form upon [their] indigest" (5.7.26). But the new king utters not one word concerning the advancing Lewis; the tenderhearted nature reflected in his tears of thanks to his nobles is touching, but it emphasizes his innocent youthfulness rather than his potential leadership. And the spectator is unlikely to have forgotten so quickly the fate of Arthur's innocent youthfulness earlier in the play.[23]

From the point of John's assertion that he has a way to win back the nobles, Shakespeare seems consciously and methodically to deconstruct the chronicle play, raising expectations only to leave them unfulfilled as the governmental process grinds to a virtual halt. It is not difficult to infer, from the extant histories and historical pageants prior to the mid 1590s—including Shakespeare's first tetralogy—that the chronicle play had assumed at least a loose kind of identity and that the spectators would have come to anticipate particular patterns or themes. Whether the earlier playwrights were directly influenced by the humanist's perception of the historian as, not a collector of facts, but "an artist who organized the facts into a coherent and attractive form"[24] (an assumption supported by Bullough's contention that *The Troublesome Reign* does just that in using the chosen facts to illustrate predetermined political and moral themes centering on the "shameful invasion of England"[25]), they most certainly—for some in the audience—were exploiting the conscious patriotism in the years immediately after the defeat of the Armada, addressing what J. P. Brockbank has called the "audience's heroic sense of community."[26]

With *King John* these inferences no longer obtain. No character on the stage possesses a significant level of perspective; that is, no one figure is in a position to have an overview of the various forces at work in the stage world. Consequently, it offers little guidance or shaping of events in such a manner as to give a particular meaning or significance to history, and the spectator individually is forced to come to terms with the welter of contradictions and conflicting ironies. In a word, the play more boldly presents political concepts that are only latently present in the earlier histories for certain perceptive members of the audience. As Eamon Grennan has recently noted, "No longer permitted the luxury of being spectators at a pageant played before them, the audience must, because of how the playwright puzzles their response, become active participants."[27] Precisely how the spectator does so either in Shakespeare's day or our own is as ambiguous as the issues of the play itself.

What is clear, in any case, is that there has been nothing before in English drama quite like Shakespeare's *King John*. If the complex political vision of the later *Henriad* bridges the gap between the stage and Renaissance academic political theory, so does *King John* bridge the gap between the two tetralogies—like a "dramatic broom with which Shakespeare sweeps away many of the no longer convincing or functional props of the historico-dramatic world of his Yorkist plays."[28] The conclusions of the future Henry plays bear witness to the development of this vision—with martial valor counterpointed by the pragmatics of survival in one, political efficiency counterpointed by a gradual but inevitable process of dehumanization in another, and the heroics of national ambition counterpointed by occasional glimpses of the price of that de-humanization and the grim reminder of the brevity of both life and empire in yet another. Again, the spectator, the director, or the critic can convincingly argue any one of several points of view in these plays, but Shakespeare's vision refuses to be bound by a particular design or ideology; it is as rich and ultimately as contra-dictory as the motivations that generate human action. If the sec-ond *Henriad* is more powerful than *John,* it is simply because the dramatic realization of that vision is less fragmented; the contrari-eties represented in *King John* by the individual characters become in the later plays internalized in the figure of Prince Hal/Henry V. An open-ended chronicle play with historical process trans-formed into human process, stripped bare of Tudor providential-ism and reduced to an individual self-interest that only in its best moments might be communally enlightened, *King John* is nothing less than a clarification for the popular stage of a new historiogra-phy dimly present in the earlier chronicle plays. The play, to bor-row a phrase from Calderwood's recent description of the "un-end" of *Lear,* gives the impression that it "has not ended but merely stopped."[29]

8
Richard II

In the fourth year of the reign of Richard II, during the Peasants' Revolt of 1381, it was, according to Holinshed's account, "dangerous among [the rebels] to be knowne for one that was lerned, and more dangerous, if any men were found with a penner and inkhorne at his side: for such seldome or neuer escaped them with life."[1] Scholars were compelled to swear that they would never teach writing again, ancient records were burned and destroyed, and many who could "commit to memorie, either any new or old records" were summarily dispatched. The commoners simplistically viewed the literate as the enemy, the oppressor, whose exploitation was responsible for the "seruitude, whereby they stood as bondmen to their lords and superiours" (2:735). But in their own way, however limited their perspective, they were making a social statement about the power of the written word controlled by authority, the full implications of which would become clear only with the simultaneous emergence in the sixteenth century of the national state and the dramatic increase in literacy. Certainly, it is ironic that these charges should emerge from the reign of Richard, which in the hands of the anonymous author of *Woodstock* and of Shakespeare was to become such a delicate subject that Elizabeth's sensitivity, presumably to the latter, is recorded directly in her comment to the antiquary William Lambarde, "I am Richard II. know ye not that? He that will forget God will also forget his benefactors,"[2] and indirectly in the omission of the deposition scene from Q_1–Q_3, the account of the events related to a performance of the play on the evening before Essex's abortive rebellion, and the imprisonment of Sir John Hayward for supposed analogies between Richard-Elizabeth and Bullingbrook-Essex in *The First Part of the Life and Reign of Henrie IV*.

These extreme reactions would hardly be warranted if we are to assume that Elizabethan spectators uniformly viewed Shakespeare's *Richard II* in the light of traditional criticism. Such interpretations tend to sanctify power by focusing on both the theoretical and pragmatic validity of monarchic government, whether, for example, through Richard's veneration for the throne, for power, and for the accoutrements of ritual despite his personal limitations, or through Bullingbrook's remorse concerning his sense of responsibility for the death of a rightful king. Either of these approaches builds to some extent upon the assumption of a fundamentally religious scheme of history "by which events evolve under a law of justice and under the ruling of God's providence."[3] Since medieval society, with the king at its head, was considered a reflection of the cosmic order ruled by God, the kingship "combines legitimacy with the assertion of a sanctity ultimately divine."[4] The playwright, according to this interpretation, is using the past didactically to glorify England and Tudor humanism; "there can be no doubt that Shakespeare believed in this almost universally accepted concept of degree, and that he accepted the Tudor doctrines of absolutism and passive obedience."[5]

The pervasive political element in each of these critical approaches is the ideology of absolutism. By appropriating religion, the monarchy assumes a sacrosanctity that marginalizes the personal abuses of the individual who holds the office and makes a virtue of obedience. Without a doubt, however, there were those in the audience who would have viewed Richard from a markedly different perspective. Recently, Graham Holderness has suggested that the political tension of the play arises from a struggle "between two antagonistic ideologies, absolutist and feudal."[6] The price of Bullingbrook's laying down his arms and kneeling in obedience before King Richard in 3.3 is stipulated in terms of a reciprocal social bond, as is his earlier plea for justice to York in 2.3 and Gaunt's deathbed advice in 2.1. Holderness concludes that Shakespeare's demystification of the theory of divine kingship in the play exposes his own ideological conviction "that a monarch rules not by the will of God but by social contract."[7] It is difficult to support such a conclusion, however, in light of the fact that Bullingbrook's own monarchic practices become literally the antithesis of the baronial rights he ostensibly had advocated earlier, a point to which I shall return. Certainly, there could hardly be a more startling example of feudal impotence than the baronial house divided against itself in act 5—York furious, his wife in tears pleading against him, their son begging for mercy from a king who, mildly amused by the scene, exercises autocratic power far more securely and efficiently than his predecessor.

Given the juxtaposition of what Holderness describes as "mutually exclusive and . . . *equally valid* forces within the ruling class,"[8] it is difficult to argue that *Richard II* consistently espouses either of the competing ideologies. Various critics, though not primarily concerned with the political implications, have described the "double-eyed . . . ambivalent quality of the play."[9] The focus at one moment is on the sanctity of a kingship, which forbids the subject to oppose the divinely ordained monarch, at another, on Richard's human mismanagement of the office coupled with his moral latitude. God's vicar on earth, capable through fits of poetic rhetoric of evoking the aura of mystery that surrounds medieval royalty as envisioned by an Elizabethan audience, is at the same time thoroughly decadent in his self-centeredness; intent upon catering to his personal pleasures, he lacks the vital concern for the security of the kingdom as well as the masculinity and the decisiveness that characterizes an effective leader. And, as for Bullingbrook, not only is he a political usurper, his motives are ambiguous from the beginning.[10] A chameleonic figure, he is apparently willing to defy the central value structures of the play for the sake of personal interests, yet he possesses all the monarchical traits the ruler lacks and, through his political acumen, is able to rescue the kingdom from lawless disaster and to save the kingship in principle, if not in person.

For dramatic purposes—and doubtless for political ones, as well—Shakespeare creates in *Richard II* a drama that, ideologically, is subject to interpretation as sympathetic either to absolutism or to feudalism or as a depiction of the uneasy but politically necessary coexistence of the two. But underlying these variables is a consistent thread that understandably would give genuine concern to Elizabeth and her public officials. For the spectator who brings to the play a particular political agenda, whatever his social status—a person, for instance, with a keen sense of social or economic oppression or, perhaps, with an indifference or an outright hostility toward royalty—might well perceive the play not as a defense of either king or baron but as a deconstruction of monarchy, aristocracy, and the principle of social hierarchy.

From such a point of view, more specifically, the play literally debunks the concept of divine right. This Richard in his own way is as much a misfit for the throne as is Shakespeare's Richard III. Crookbacked Richard at the very least does not glorify his villainy in the name of God and his own right; indeed, he scrupulously avoids even the mention of the deity in his oration to his soldiers at Bosworth Field. Richard II, to the contrary, touts himself as an embodiment of the religio-political principle of divine right, constantly invoking God and legal doctrine to validate his political power. Through such actions he becomes virtually an anti-king, in practice desecrating every value that he espouses. That is, the utter separation of the principle from Richard's every action drains all life from the concept and leaves it a hollow mockery that spectators so attuned can see as a tool for political containment.[11]

Of the five separate occasions in the play on which the concept is invoked, the first two depict flagrant crimes provided state protection by the doctrine. Richard's uncles clearly see a need to move against the abuses of royal power but consider themselves bound by the divinity that hedges the kingship. Gaunt, more specifically, considers the concept a device to protect the king from either legal process or personal vengeance; Richard, guilty of the murder of his uncle Gloucester, stands above the law by virtue of his political position. The widowed Duchess of Gloucester urges Gaunt to revenge his brother's death:

> Ah, Gaunt, his blood was thine! That bed, that womb,
> That mettle, that self mould, that fashioned thee,
> Made him a man; and thou thou livest and breathest,
> Yet art thou slain in him.
>
> (1.2.22–25)[12]

To both the call of blood and the call of justice, however, Gaunt poses protective political doctrine. Since Richard is "God's substitute" (37), "His deputy anointed" (38), heaven alone must revenge the crime; "for I may never lift / An angry arm against His minister" (40–41). The tone is equally critical in act 2 as York berates Richard for his intention to appropriate Gaunt's estate to the crown, effectively robbing the exiled Bulingbrook of wealth and title. York notes explicitly that the cornerstone of divine right is the law of primogeniture; to strip that right from the highest nobles in the land is to undermine the foundation of the throne itself:

> Take Herford's rights away, and take from Time
> His charters and his customary rights;
> Let not to-morrow then ensue to-day;
> Be not thyself; for how art thou a king
> But by fair sequence and succession?
>
> (2.1.195–99)

Richard, in a word, is protected by a doctrine that he abuses at will, yet specifically approves as a sacred trust when he returns from Ireland and senses a genuine danger from Bullingbrook. He speaks of touching "my kingdom" with "royal hands," reiterating that none "Can wash the balm off from an anointed king" (3.2.5, 11, 55). But, again, the context mocks the vaunted claim. In a moment of military crisis he reeks of maudlin sentimentality, both weeping and smiling like "a long-parted mother with her child" (3.2.8) as he greets the earth and admonishes it to place obstacles in the usurper's path. Indeed, his behavior is so unkingly that one of his staunchest supporters, the bishop of Carlisle, must urge him to act boldly in his own behalf—and in a manner that will lend validity to the religio-political concept. Through his smug response that no "worldly men" can "depose / The deputy elected by the Lord" (56–57), however, he in effect justifies his own inactivity; if "heaven still guards the right," then he need not worry. By the end of the scene he, in a complete reversal, has collapsed into a despair that reveals his kingly claims as little more than posturing.

At Flint Castle the pattern repeats itself. Richard at the outset, speaking from the turret to Bullingbrook in the court below, chastizes his cousin for failure to bend his knee before a "lawful king" appointed to his "stewardship" by the "hand of God" (3.3.74, 78, 77). He warns Bullingbrook that "God omnipotent / Is mustering in his clouds on our behalf / Armies of pestilence" that will protect the "sacred handle of [his] sceptre" (85–87, 80). Yet within moments his resolve disappears as he laments to Aumerle that his grief is greater than his title and to Bullingbrook that he will descend "like glist'ring Phaeton, / Wanting the manage of unruly jades" (178–79). Within a few more moments he, without even a verbal fight, has become a political prisoner: "Your own is yours, and I am yours, and all" (197).

Whether, then, for crimes of commission or of omission justified in the name of God, Richard, in his abuse of divine right, can hardly be described as a king by right and the play as a defense of the medieval doctrine. Indeed, the final occasion on which the concept is invoked baldly reveals that it is servant to political power, appropriated when convenient, and repudiated at will. At the moment Henry announces at Westminster his intention to assume the kingship, the bishop of Carlisle thunders that Hereford is a foul traitor to Richard, "the figure of God's majesty / His captain, steward, deputy, elect, / Anointed, crowned" (4.1.125–27). For his defense of the doctrine he is peremptorily arrested and charged with high treason, and yet in a masterstroke of irony a few lines earlier, Henry has appropriated it to himself, proclaiming that "In *God's* name [emphasis mine] I'll ascend the regal throne" (113). God, divine right, and religion, all are revealed as little more than doctrinal mechanisms by which a ruler, acting entirely in his own self-interest, can legitimize himself and thereby lay claim to obedience from both the aristocracy and the commoners.

At the same time, the play depicts a monarchy methodically attempting to consolidate its absolutist powers by stripping away the rights from an aristocracy that is struggling to retain its privileged position within a feudal hierarchy. When Richard casts down his warder at the lists in Coventry—"with words that describe a rebellion rather than a formal tournament"[13]—he thereby denies to Bullingbrook and Mowbray the right of trial by combat. This action reflects a struggle already almost two centuries old in Europe. Obviously, from any king's point of view, a custom that permits an individual to determine right from wrong and himself to act as judge and jury not only privileges a particular class but also severely undermines the royal prerogative. Historically, however, any advance in royal power for a time had to come through a compromise that would continue to grant a nobleman the "right to wear his sword and to uphold his personal honour in the duel."[14] Both the Neopolitan code of Frederick II in 1231 and the German Imperial code (the Kayser-Recht) of about the same time attempted sharply to limit the charges to which the wager of battle might apply; in 1248 James I of Aragon prohibited it altogether as a custom "reprehensible both as a tempting of God and as a source of perpetual injustice."[15] If European monarchs more and more successfully were attacking this aristocratic privilege, however, the Barons' Wars and Magna Charta inhibited the evolution of theocratic autocracy in England and delayed the major struggle for a time. Near the end of the fourteenth century, for example, when the custom was virtually obsolete in France, Thomas, duke of Gloucester, "dedicated to his nephew Richard II, a treatise detailing elaborately the practice followed in the Marshal's court with respect to judicial duels."[16]

One of the means through which English rulers countered such opposition was by extending the laws of treason, not only to increase their general sphere of influence but also, in more practical terms, to secure for the crown the escheats of the greater number of nobles adjudged guilty of such a crime.[17] The treason act of 1352 represented a temporary reconciliation on the matter between Edward III and his baronage, carefully distinguishing between high treason (crimes against "the King's person and his regality") and petty treason (actions to be tried as felonies).[18] Specifically, according to one historian, the "main purpose of the statute of 1352 was by means of statutory definition to prevent the recurrence of the reckless charges and arbitrary punishments which had ruined so many noble families in the reign of Edward II."[19] A century later, however, the problem was as acute as ever. As one Kentishman observed in 1450, "Item they say when the kynge wulle shall be traytours and when he wull schalle be none; and that aperuthe wele hiderto."[20]

Richard II was especially guilty of painting the label of treason with a remarkably broad brush. In 1381, for example, at the time of the Peasants' Revolt, hundreds were perfunctorily executed on grounds of high treason, stirring little opposition from his nobles in these particular cases only because it was the lower class that suffered. But again the charge had become fair game for extending the royal prerogative, as evidenced in his successor's reign, when Lollards "were often accused of the treason of *imagining* the king's death."[21]

The duel between Bullingbrook and Mowbray relates directly to this historical struggle. As Holinshed records, each in the parliament of 1398 accused the other of high treason:

> Henrie duke of Hereford accused Thomas Mowbraie duke of Norfolke, of certeine words which he should vtter in talke had betwixt them, as they rode togither latelie before betwixt London and Brainford, sounding highlie to the kings dishonor. And, for further proofe thereof, he presented a supplication to the king, wherein he appealed the duke of Norfolke in field of battell, for a traitor, false and disloiall to the king, and enimie vnto the realme.... Then the duke of Norfolke being asked what he said to this, he answered: "Right deere lord, with your fauour that I make answer vnto your coosine here, I saie (your reuerence saued) that Henrie of Lancaster duke of Hereford, like a false and disloiall traitor as he is, dooth lie, in that he hath or shall say to me otherwise than well." (2:844)

Six weeks later, at Windsor, Bullingbrook specifically reminded Richard of the noble's privilege to settle such matters by knightly combat, reaffirming his charge of treason against his adversary: "Right deere lord, they are my woords; and hereof I require right, and the battell against him" (2:845).

Such countercharges of high treason played directly into Richard's hands. Most obviously, it gave him the opportunity to exact vengeance against the two remaining lords appellant, who had defeated the king's army at Radcor Bridge in Oxfordshire and who, in effect, had ruled the realm for a year in 1388–89. Richard had already dealt with three—exiling Warwick, beheading Arundel, and apparently murdering Gloucester; and, even though he had accepted reconciliation with Bullingbrook and Mowbray, the relationship was at best tentative.

By law, in duels involving an accusation of high treason, the "vanquished party, whether he was the appellant or the defendant, was disarmed in the lists and drawn behind a horse in the charge of the Marshal to the place of execution, where he was beheaded or hanged."[22] Richard, however, who as king solely possessed such authority, abruptly canceled the proceedings; and, after consulting for two hours with his council, banished both parties—Mowbray for life and Bullingbrook for a period of ten years (later shortened to six). That Richard's decision to prohibit the duel was both unplanned and unanticipated is suggested by the elaborate and expensive preparations for the event. According to Holinshed, the opposing lords came "in great arraie, accompanied with the lords and gentlemen of their linages"; Richard "caused a sumptuous scaffold or theater, and roiall listes there to be erected and prepared"; and the "king had there aboue ten thousand men in armour, least some fraie or tumult might rise amongst his nobles, by quarrelling or partaking" (2:846, 847). And certainly there were immediate personal ramifications that also suggest Richard's action was precipitate; Norfolk, for example, was "in hope (as writers record) that he should have been borne out in the matter by the king, which when it fell out otherwise, it greeued him not a little" (2:848).

On the other hand, the long-range political ramifications suggest that Richard's action could not have been more precisely calculated in advance. By rescinding the right to a combat by duel without pardoning the adversaries, the charges of treason technically remained in force. Consequently, when Gaunt died, within less than a year, Richard

seized into his hands all the goods that belonged to him, and also receiued all the rents and reuenues of his lands which ought to haue descended vnto the duke of Hereford by lawfull inheritance, in reuoking his letters pattents, which he had granted to him before, by vertue whereof he might make his attorneis generall to sue liuerie for him, of any manner of inheritances or possessions that might from thenceforth fall vnto him, and that his homage might be respited, with making reasonable fine: whereby it was euident, that the king meant his vtter undoing. (2:849)

In a word, Richard extended the authority of the parliamentary committee appointed to handle the treason charges arising out of the quarrel between Bullingbrook and Mowbray—in effect, extended the charge of treason against Bullingbrook—and thereby revoked the "license enabling Bullingbrook's attorneys to claim the Lancastrian inheritance on behalf of the exiled heir."[23]

Shakespeare understandably shortens and collapses these events, but the textual strategy suggests that he might well have perceived such an ultimate design in Holinshed's account. Richard in the opening lines makes it specifically clear to all assembled that Bullingbrook and Mowbray intend "to appeal each other of high treason" (1.1.27). In speaking to Gaunt about Hereford's charge he selects words calculated to exacerbate the situation by tending to diminish Bullingbrook—"to *boy* him—and to stress Gaunt's responsibility for his son's good behavior."[24] Then, for well over one hundred lines he permits the adversaries to engage in dialogue that grows increasingly tense and combative, interrupting them only briefly to ask what charges each brings against the other and to assure Mowbray that he is free to voice his grievance despite Hereford's royal blood. Only when Mowbray officially requests that the day of their duel be established does Richard, who in effect has encouraged the public statement of their argument, suggest a reconciliation—at a point when it can be assumed that each will be most staunchly determined to fight, whether to protect his "spotless reputation" (178) or his noble image "in [his] father's eyes" (188). What has so often been interpreted as vacillation—both the ostensible attempt to reconcile the adversaries and later the refusal to allow the duel to continue—is, in this reading, a shrewd attempt to strengthen the crown against two of its most powerful barons. When Richard proclaims that his reasons for disallowing the trial by combat are to prevent "civil wounds" from "wak[ing] our peace" and "mak[ing] us wade even in our own kindred's blood" (1.3.128, 132, 138), he has masterfully transformed personal vengeance against the last lords appellant into an act of statesmanship and princely concern. In this scene, even his later reduction of Bullingbrook's exile is hardly an indecisive act emanating either from compassion or fear; it is a final affirmation of royal prerogative, a calculated gamble on the fragility of Gaunt's health.

While admittedly the most spectacular, Richard's quasi-legal seizure of Bullingbrook's inheritance is only one of a series of power plays throughout the drama. Richard's decision in 1.4 to pursue the war in Ireland, for example, is purely unilateral, as is his plan to sell the right to taxation for ready cash and his use of blank charters to raise additional revenues. Disgruntled nobles, complaining that such actions have lost the hearts of both commoners and aristocrats, fear the king will seize upon false information to "prosecute / 'Gainst us, our lives, our children, and our heirs" (2.1.144–45). Nor is Bullingbrook's record any better. He gains the monarchy through the criminal action of violating his banishment, clearly promising eventual material reward to those who support him:

> All my treasury
> Is yet but unfelt thanks, which more enrich'd
> Shall be your love and labor's recompense.
>
> . . . .
>
> Evermore thank's the exchequer of the poor,
> Which, till my infant fortune comes to years,
> Stands for my bounty.
>
> (2.3.60–62, 65–67)

(Holinshed, incidentally, records a more immediate reward of sorts in that Bullingbrook "vndertooke to cause the paiment of taxes and tallages [feudal payments] to be laid downe [revoked]" [2:853]). His uncle, York, brands him a traitor, not only for violating his banishment, but also for leading a military entourage across England; and those in the rebel army are proclaimed guilty of "gross rebellion and detested treason" (2.3.109). Bullingbrook's next action, at Bristol Castle, is to condemn Bushy and Green to death without trial.[25] (Holinshed reports that they were "found guiltie of treason, for misgouerning the king and realme" [2:854]). At Flint Castle he vows "to lay [his] arms and power" at Richard's feet, "Provided that [his] banishment repeal'd / And lands restor'd again be fully granted" (3.3.39, 40–41); he even kneels before Richard and swears that he "come[s] but for [his] own" (196). Yet, even though Richard freely grants that Bullingbrook's demands "shall be accomplish'd without contradiction" (124), the king has been arrested by the end of the scene.[26] At Westminister Bullingbrook denies trial by combat to no fewer than five of his nobles,[27] after which he ascends the throne totally without concern for parliamentary concurrence.[28] Once king, his use of the charge of treason to eliminate political enemies—whether within the church (the bishop of Carlisle, the abbot of Westminister) or within the baronage (Oxford, Salisbury, Kent, Brocas, Seely)—has an all-too-familiar ring. And his public act of banishing Exton as a means of distancing himself from Richard's murder (even though Exton claims "From your own mouth, my lord, did I this deed" [5.6.37]) is pointedly analogous to Richard's attempt to distance himself from Gloucester's murder by banishing Mowbray.

From this perspective *Richard II* reflects from beginning to end the inherent struggle for power and control within the privileged class, the willingness to resort to treachery and deceit to gain political power, and the cunning to legitimize actions by manipulating religion and law to the service of self-interests. The lower class has only a shadow existence, present only as an object of exploitation and scornful allusion by both sides. Richard mockingly refers to the "slaves," "poor craftsmen," "oyster-wench[es]," and "draymen" courted by Bullingbrook (1.4.27, 28, 31, 32); Scroop, to the "White beards . . . [with] thin and hairless scalps," the "boys, with women's voices," and the "distaff women" who support the rebellion (3.2.112, 113, 118); Bullingbrook, callously to the "crimson tempest" that will rain "from the wounds of slaughtered Englishmen" (3.3.46, 44); Richard, pompously to the "ten thousand bloody crowns of mothers' sons" who will change England's complexion to "scarlet indignation" (3.3.96, 99). Pawns in the power plays of the aristocracy, the commoners have no voice in their own destiny, though obviously they are subject to paying a hideous price in life and limb. The play, then, not privileging one political view over another, is ideologically open-ended, forcing a mimetic negotiation of what Stephen Greenblatt has recently described as "an unresolved struggle between competing representational discourses"[29] Shakespeare's refusal to provide the comfort of fundamental emotional and intellectual identification with a single political tenet—coupled with the consistent denigration of the entire political process—"works to implicate the audience in the action and to transgress the comfortable demarcation between stage and audience."[30] The result is a seemingly conscious and methodic deconstruction of any sense of providentialism; the aura and mystique of royalty are transformed to the grim realities of secular interaction, reducing government and society to the chaos of individual machination at worst and an unstable nexus of conflicting self-interests at best.

9
The *Henriad*

Gary Taylor recently wrote that "every dramatist constructs a hypothetical audience, and that the success or failure of his intentions depends on the relations between his real and his hypothetical spectators."[1] The lesson of the chronicle plays is that for Shakespeare and his fellow playwrights such a hypothetical audience was not a monolithic social unit but a disparate group whose responses were based on individual emotional, intellectual, and political interests. Certainly, by deleting lines, by altering setting and costume, or by utilizing topical symbolism, a modern director can emphasize specific themes and thereby encourage a particular kind of response. The Olivier film version of *Henry V* in 1944, for example, made savage cuts in the text (some seventeen hundred lines), removing virtually every doubt from the hero's mind in order to create a splendidly patriotic pageant; the Old Vic production in 1951, directed by Glen B. Shaw, likewise eliminated all negative aspects of Henry's character and magnified the unattractiveness of his opponents. On the other hand, the Royal Shakespeare Company's antiwar production in 1964, like that of Michael Kahn for the American Shakespeare Theater in 1969, or that of the Santa Cruz Shakespeare Festival in 1984, with its pervasive images of Vietnam and Nicaragua, deemphasized the traditional heroics. "The martial events leading up to and including the battle of Agincourt [were] presented as bloody, clobbering and unpleasant";[2] the ragged army and desperately fatigued leader epitomized not the heroics but the horrors of war. The Kott-inspired *Lear* of Peter Brook also catered to timely sentiment, as have recent feminist productions of such plays as *The Taming of the Shrew* and *Love's Labor's Lost*, and a politically charged, anti-imperialistic version of *The Tempest.*

Such efforts never fully succeed, however, in regimenting a univocal reaction in any stage world beyond melodrama. So long as characters are not purely good or evil, so long as shreds of ambiguity remain in the motivations of the stage figures and the interactions, so long as the spectator is forced to play some sort of interpretive role—disparate views and disparate responses will obtain. It would have been enlightening, for example, to interview 1987 theatergoers at the Barbican in London, where they saw a trendy, updated version of *Romeo and Juliet* in which the closing scene focused on a reunion of the two rival families that would bring a return of economic prosperity to Verona and in which the nurse and Friar Lawrence were touted as veritable heroes. For some in the audience the tragic was, paradoxically, blended with the comic into a tone suggestive of mercantile joy and celebration. Presumably, a professorial aversion to such an interpretation could be largely attributable to a long-standing familiarity with the young lovers' ill-advised but affecting struggle for happiness in a cruel and hostile environment, but many unfamiliar with the play apparently sensed a similar disgust with or indifference to the action center stage, as their eyes and emotions wandered to a dim, almost forgotten corner where the protagonists' bodies lay in neglected state. Perhaps the most compelling recent example is the sharply divided response to the portrayal of Isabella in a Stratford production of *Measure For Measure* several years ago. A stridently independent figure from the opening scenes, she confirmed her genderic political stance by momentarily gazing in amazement when the Duke proposed in the final scene; then amazement evolved into obvious repulsion as, turning her back upon the aristocratic suitor, she stalked off stage with a clearly haughty finality. Whatever divisions the spectators experienced on patriarchal and feminist grounds throughout the play were exacerbated in that final moment, which evoked an almost equal mingling of hisses and applause. Derek Cohen is surely correct in asserting that the audience, as the "willing captive of drama's most private moments and thus the willing possessor of the secret thoughts and desires of characters in a play . . . becomes, perforce, a collaborator in the action."[3] But it is dangerously reductionistic to assume that such collaboration necessarily results in any kind of uniformity of response.

Richard II, as discussed earlier, features a series of power plays through which the central figure attempts to enhance the authority of the monarchy by progressively restricting the rights of the nobility. These actions ultimately plunge England into civil war, a period in any age in which civil law bows to brute force in a struggle between the traditional sanctions of power and those who

come to envision that power as inalterably oppressive and tyrannical. Whatever the outcome of such a struggle, the political regime
that survives must inevitably employ a strategy for authorizing
power through which, from the public point of view, there is a
reinvestment of the sanctions of authority. Shakespeare's *Henriad*
may indeed focus for some spectators on Henry's rueful realization that only force can support force as his violation of the
religio-political traditions of kingship thrusts him into confrontation with continuing rebellion in Scotland, Wales, and northern
England—or on the increasing paralysis of will resulting from
Henry's sense of guilt for deposing a divinely ordained monarch—or on the education of Prince Hal as he practices the various roles that will enable him to be a successful ruler and that
culminate in his military victories in France and in his political
acumen in securing the dynasty through marriage with the foreign princess. Such views, as noted by critics from Tillyard to
Reed,[4] support the fundamental assumptions of the Tudor myth.
For others in the audience, however, the perceived political ideology might have been sharply different. For whatever else it might
be about, the *Henriad* depicts the Lancastrian struggle to maintain
power and, more importantly, to invest it with a pragmatic and
theoretical acceptability. A lesson in realpolitik, these three plays
depict from one perspective the transformation of England from
the petty brawls of internecine strife to a nation unified in a righteous struggle against arrogant French imperialism and lay bare,
from another, the strategies of political absolutism; as wily
usurper becomes revered monarch and dissolute son becomes
embodiment of royal idolatry, the stage confirms the "Machiavellian hypothesis of the origin of princely power in force and fraud
even as it draws its audience irresistibly toward the celebration of
that power."[5]
    The title figure, appearing in only nine of thirty-eight scenes
in *1,2 Henry IV*, is nevertheless central to this theme. David
Bevington has recently remarked that, "because he constantly
masks his personal and political self, King Henry is a hard character to read."[6] The difficulty arises not from any inconsistency in
character but from the fact that publicly he is constantly playing
a carefully scripted role; everything that he says and does in public is designed to construct the image of a judicious and courageous ruler. Indeed, on his deathbed he admits to Hal that "all
[his] reign hath been but as a scene / Acting that argument" (*2
Henry IV*, 4.5.197–98).[7] On occasion his tone is almost paternal as

he addresses the past wounds of his nation. In the opening scene, for example, he proclaims that

> No more the thirsty entrance of this soil
> Shall daub her lips with her own children's blood,
> No more shall trenching war channel her fields,
> Nor bruise her flow'rets with the armed hoofs
> Of hostile paces.
>
> (pt. 1, 1.1.5–9)

Those who recently closed in "civil butchery" shall now "March all one way and be no more oppos'd / Against acquaintance kindred, and allies" (13, 15–16). The same conciliatory tone surfaces in 5.1 as, ostensibly motivated by the love he has for his people in both his and the rebel army, he offers terms of peace to Hotspur (104–8).

On other occasions Henry displays qualities of vigorous leadership, whether in seeking advice from his counselors (pt. 1, 1.1.30–33; pt. 2, 3.1.1–3, 35–36) or in his alacrity in establishing a plan of battle and dispatching his forces to combat (pt. 1, 3.2.170–80, 5.5.34–44); even in sickness his paramount concern appears to be adequate preparation for the defense of his kingdom (pt. 2, 3.1.93–96, 4.4.5–7). There are public displays of courage, too, as in his ordering Worcester from the council chamber and facing down the fiery Hotspur with the peremptory command, "Send me your prisoners with the speediest means, / Or you shall hear in such a kind from me / As will displease you" (pt. 1, 1.3.120–22); on the battlefield he urges his forces to fight bravely, and he himself readily confronts the Scottish Douglas, though his martial feats prove less effective than his verbal threats and he must be rescued by his son (pt. 1, 5.4.29–34, 47–50). At times his political judgment publicly appears to be keen, as in his conviction that Mortimer has joined in league with Glendower rather than being overcome in battle; the fact that Hotspur privately also considers this to be true (1.3.280–81) makes Henry's assumption less remarkable, though it does not diminish the force of his public pronouncement. Or consider his offer of full redress of grievances to the rebel army rather than risking the entire campaign on single combat between Hal and Hotspur (pt. 1, 5.1.103–10); the political strategy of this action is especially clever, since he is able to cover any uncertainties about Hal's ability to defeat Hotspur with an offer of peace that, to all appear-

ances, is motivated by princely magnanimity. In short, a careful
examination of Henry's actions reveals that, for every strategy of
legitimation, the play provides "an alternative strategy of subversion . . . encourag[ing] the spectator to interrogate the state's motives and purposes."[8]

Perhaps most significant in cultivating the image of national
leader, Henry uses devices of both appropriation and containment, simultaneously appropriating religion to his political cause
and isolating his adversaries as alien to God and human brother-
hood. The ploy of the crusade to the Holy Land, for example,
is virtually an exemplum on Machiavelli's text that any effective
ruler utilizes religion to bend the people to his authority.[9] Invoking such images as "sepulchre of Christ," "blessed cross," "holy
fields," "blessed feet," and "bitter cross" for a venture that he full
well knows will never come to reality, he is able not only to align
himself with God's cause but also, at the same time, to brand the
rebels as the "other," creatures of evil who prevent this crusade
in the name of Christ (pt. 1, 1.1.19–27 passim, 101–2). "Legiti-
mat[ing] inequality and exploitation by representing the social
order which perpetuates these things as . . . decreed by God or
simply natural,"[10] Henry rallies his troops at Shrewsbury in the
assurance that "God [will] befriend us as our cause is just!" (pt.
1, 5.1.120); and, following the battle, he publicly castigates the rebellion as satanic in his pronouncement to Worcester that many
on both sides would still be alive "If like a Christian thou hadst
truly borne / Betwixt our armies true intelligence" (5.5.9–10).
Even in his illness he reiterates the pledge to lead the youth of
England to "higher fields, / And draw no swords but what are
sanctified" after God successfully ends "this debate that bleedeth
at our doors" (pt. 2, 4.4.3–4, 2). And he reinforces this spiritual
instigation to obedience through what Stephen Greenblatt describes as "the arousal of anxiety" or "managed insecurity,"[11] well-
timed displays of power, such as public executions, lest one be
tempted to forget the physical price of rebellion (pt. 1, 5.5.14; pt.
2, 4.4.84–85).

That all of this is, indeed, a carefully scripted role on Henry's
part, built on the Machiavellian premise that the ruler must take
care to maintain the dignity of his position, which should never
suffer diminution for any reason,[12] Shakespeare makes undenia-
bly clear through the king's occasional private moments with the
heir apparent. The absence of father/son bonding has often been
remarked upon. Henry, in fact, in part 1 seems to attempt to sub-
limate his fear of providential retribution into an adversarial rela-

tionship with Hal; "[f]or some displeasing service I have done," "[t]o punish my mistreadings," "God will have it so," breeding "revengement and a scourge for me . . . in thy passages of life" (pt. 1, 3.2.4–8 passim). It is somehow as if he believes that he need fear no divine political recriminations so long as Hal plagues him. He is exasperated, above all, that the son refuses to play the proper role as heir apparent; and this obsessive concern for public image prompts him to insist that a ruler must be "seldom seen" so that appearance begets wonder; one, further, must be "dress'd . . . in such humility" that it will "pluck allegiance from men's hearts" (3.2.46, 51–52). In part 2, frankly acknowledging the scene he has consciously enacted throughout his reign (4.5. 197–98), he admits that he has come to the crown by "indirect crook'd ways" (184) and that his proclamation of a crusade to Jerusalem was a "purely machiavellian"[13] ruse "to busy giddy minds / With foreign quarrels" (213–14), the manufacturing of a common foe in order to reduce tensions and minimize factions within the kingdom. What some view as a humanizing moment, in which the spectator shares the agony of the guilt-ridden king and the pressures of royalty, others view quite differently as a glimpse beneath the actor's mask at the raw motives by which he dispassionately attempts to legitimize a usurped throne.

From such a perspective Hal, in many ways, is a psychological double of his father. If Henry's role is one of a subtle manipulation of appearance that becomes apparent to the spectator only well into the plays, Hal announces his guise in a soliloquy in his first scene on stage. Moreover, while Henry after his usurpation is concerned with appearances above all, Hal is determined to flout traditional expectations, proclaiming that his intention is to effect a transformation of image at the moment of his ascendancy that, in its own way, will attract even more attention (and hence capture greater admiration and reverence) than his father's behavior. The legend of the madcap youth was, of course, one of the most popular of Shakespeare's age, the germ found in the chronicles and the fuller development in *The Famous Victories of Henry V*. Of Prince Henry's company, Holinshed reports only that a "great resort of people came to his house, so that the court was nothing furnished with such a traine as dailie followed the prince" (3:53)[14] and elsewhere that "[i]ndeed he was youthfullie giuen, growne to audacity, and had chosen him companions agreeable to his age; with whom he spent the time in such recreations, exercises, and delights as he fansied" (3:54); in "Henrie the Fift, Prince of Wales" the historian further notes that "aforetime he had made himselfe a companion vnto misrulie mates of dissolute order and life" (3:61). Three incidents relative to his behavior and the troubled relationship with his father are recorded at some length. In one, concerning his determination "to put on him the shape of a new man," Hal retains the "cheefe iustice" who earlier had committed him to the "ward" for an incident in which one of his "minions (vpon desert) [was sent] to prison." The second incident, discussed earlier in connection with *The Famous Victories*, relates a visit to court to challenge slanderous charges against him, at which time he gives the king a dagger and offers his throat to be cut if the father mistrusts him; the consequence is a moving and apparently permanent reconciliation between the two. The third incident, involving Prince Henry's taking the crown when he assumes his father to be dead, prompts no sharp exchange, only the king's remark "with a great sigh," "Well faire sonne . . . what right I had to it, God knoweth. . . . I commit all to God, and remember you to doo well" (3:57).

It is important to note, furthermore, that in Holinshed the legend of the wayward prince is politically innocuous:

But yet (it should seeme by the report of some writers) that his behauiour was not offensiue or at least tending to the damage of anie bodie; sith he had a care to auoid dooing of wrong, and to tender his affections within the tract of vertue, whereby he opened vnto himselfe a redie passage of good liking among the prudent sort, and was beloued of such as could discerne his disposition, which was in no degree so excessiue, as that he deserued in such vehement manner to be suspected." (3:55)

Both Shakespeare and the anonymous author of *The Famous Victories*, on the other hand, adapt and flesh out this legend for ideological purposes. From this perspective Hal's actions as heir apparent denigrate the monarchy and reflect the plight of the commoners in such a society. Hal's crass disregard for the traditional ritualistic values of the crown emphasizes his concern only for personal pleasure and for the material benefits that accrue from a privileged position above the law. The result, for the spectators inclined to this view, is a demystification of the royal house and an exposure of the corruption at its center.

However much traditional criticism lauds Hal's initial soliloquy in part 1 as an indication that he is fully mindful of his ultimate responsibilities and that he consciously and methodically is educating himself for the task, for example, the less sympathetic spec-

tator inevitably perceives him as smugly arrogant, especially in
the presumptuous comparison of his loose behavior abruptly cast
aside with the sun suddenly emerging from behind dark clouds
and provoking great wonder. His frank intention to "show more
goodly and attract more eyes" (1.2.214) is certainly no less calculated a role than that of his father, and the fact that such action
involves the manipulation of those beneath him in social standing
and hence with little or no recourse he seems totally to disregard.[15] There is, moreover, a suggestion of blatant rationalization,
both in the opening speech, in which he justifies dissolute behavior in the name of later reformation, and in part 2, in which—in
the face of Poins's quip that not many sons would act so frivolously
with their father ill and dying—he retorts, "Let the end try the
man; . . . in every thing the purpose must weigh with the folly"
(2.2.47, 175–76).

Of Hal's flagrant exploitation of those around him surely the
most celebrated instance is Falstaff, who—comically forewarned
in part 1 (2.4.481)—is abruptly abandoned in part 2 (5.5.47–72).
Whether one considers Falstaff a free spirit or a depraved para-
site, it is traditional to speak of Hal's learning from him, among
other things, the dangers of moral latitude.[16] Actually, that initial
soliloquy forces the spectators to question whether Hal really has
anything to learn from his companion about the skill of moral
evasion or whether he really considers the fat knight as any kind
of tutor. More likely he simply enjoys Falstaff's company until the
moment when such companionship is no longer politically feasi-
ble, and as a kind of moral salve he sporadically reminds himself
and the spectators that such a time is inevitable. Falstaff, of
course, is only one of several banished by Hal. Poins in some ways
seems to be an even closer companion. Nearer in age to the
prince, he is the mastermind in the plot to counterrob Falstaff,
convincing Hal to take part and assuring him of its success. He
is the constant companion in part 2, as well, so much so that it
arouses the jealousy of the fat reprobate, who attempts to alienate
the two by sending word that Poins is noising it about that the
prince intends to marry his sister, Nell. Disguised as waiters at the
Boar's Head tavern, he and Hal mock Falstaff in his amorous encounter with Doll Tearsheet. While Poins, in a word, shares Hal's
close confidence throughout the plays, we hear nothing of him
after the ascension, only the king's ominous declaration that he
has banished all of his "misleaders" (pt. 2, 5.5.64). Reaction from
these erstwhile companions is limited but poignant. Of Falstaff,
Hostess Quickly reports that "the King hath kill'd his heart"

(*Henry V* 2.1.88); Nym, that "the King hath run bad humors on the knight" (121–22); and Pistol, that Falstaff's "heart is fracted and corroborate" (124).

The political cunning that Hal displays in his association with these low-life figures is his realization that he must subordinate emotion and affection to the quest for power. He exploits them for their companionship at one moment, then discards them without sentiment when it is politically prudent. In another sense, Hal also exploits Hotspur. If at Shrewsbury he is intent upon killing the northern youth as the leader of the enemy forces, his obsession takes shape long before the rebellion. As early as act 2 he is well aware of the reputation of Northumberland's son:

> I am not yet of Percy's mind, the Hotspur of the North, he that kills me some six or seven dozen of Scots at a breakfast, washes his hands, and says to his wife, "Fie upon this quiet life! I want work." "O my sweet Harry," says she, "how many hast thou kill'd to-day?" "Give my roan horse a drench," says he, and answers, "Some fourteen," an hour after; "a trifle, a trifle." (pt. 1, 2.4.101–8)

And his pledge to his father to "redeem all [his shortcomings] on Percy's head," to make Hotspur "exchange / His glorious deeds for my indignities" (3.2.132, 145–46), is delivered at a time when we, and presumably Hal, know only that Hotspur is one of six potential commanders (see 2.4.335–59). Percy, in other words, is Hal's "factor" from the outset, just as in other ways Falstaff, Poins, even his father and later the Lord Chief Justice are his factors, figures to be manipulated and used in any number of ways to enhance the prince's image and fortune.

From an ideological perspective, then, both King Henry and Prince Hal, each in his own way, are determined to secure and legitimize power, and the two at times work directly at cross purposes. As Leonard Tennenhouse observes, "Together these chronicle history plays demonstrate . . . that authority goes to the contender who can seize hold of the symbols and signs legitimizing authority and wrest them from his rivals to make them serve his own interests."[17] Tennenhouse contends that Hal is able to appropriate to himself the "popular energy embodied in carnival" and thereby to gain the spectators' sympathy and support as a "source of power contrary to that inhering in genealogy."[18] The contention here, to the contrary, is that both the author of *The Famous Victories* and Shakespeare consciously employ carnivalesque elements, not to legitimize Hal, but, as Michael Bristol puts it, to "oppose the 'official' culture. . . . [Through] laughter, irony, humor, elements of self-parody . . . carnival inserts into these structures an indeterminacy, a certain semiotic openendedness, a living contact with unfinished, still-evolving contemporary reality."[19]

Falstaff, indeed, is funny; his antics undercut the austerity of King Henry in the mock confrontation between father and son (pt. 1, 2.4.376–481); and his catechism on honor, his feigned death, and his wounding of Hotspur's corpse at Shrewsbury (5.1.129–41; 5.3.32–39; 5.4.111–29) counterpoint the bravado of honor and battlefield heroics, as do his late arrival and his mock-heroic capture of Sir John Coleville at Gaultree Forest (pt. 2, 4.3.1–29). In the final analysis, however, all such carnivalesque characters serve to denigrate the heir apparent, whether through the condescending attitude that culminates in his calculated, predetermined rejection of them or through the antimonarchic comments and actions they evoke from him throughout the play. The humor ultimately fails to cover the egregious monarchical dislocation of Hal's loitering away his time in a London pub while the kingdom boils with insurrection. And, jest or not, when the king's son seizes in highway robbery "money of the King's" en route "to the King's exchequer" (pt. 1, 2.2.54, 55)—or when the prince dallies with a "join'd-stool" as the throne, a leaden dagger for a sceptre, and a cushion for the crown of England (2.4.380–82)—the symbols of disorder have permeated the very center of the kingdom. Moreover, the jest completely evaporates as Hal faces the sheriff in pursuit of Falstaff:

> The man I do assure you is not here,
> For I myself at this time have employ'd him.
> And, sheriff, I will engage my word to thee
> That I will by to-morrow dinner-time
> Send him to answer thee.
>
> (512–16)

Lying with an absolutely straight face, Hal is indeed in training for whatever duplicity the royal office will require of him. Nor is it likely that commoners in the audience would find much humor in his crass manipulation of the drawer, Francis, who— both in years and in social status—is no equal for the prince. Hal's laughter at the lad's bewilderment and intimidation is rather like that of the village bully, a "containment of subversion" at the individual level.[20] Furthermore, entrusting Falstaff with a charge of foot (which the fat rogue would prefer to be a charge of horse [whores]) and with money to impress (which in bribery he "mis-use[s] . . . damnably, . . . [getting] in exchange of one hundred and fifty soldiers, three hundred and odd pounds" [4.2.12–14]) may provoke a chuckle, but it hardly conceals the fact that such action compromises the security of the kingdom. The pitiful and sickly lot that Falstaff assembles he excuses as "food for powder, food for powder, they'll fill a pit as well as better" (65–67), and their leader is as good as his word: "I have led my ragamuffins where they are pepper'd; there's not three of my hundred and fifty left alive, and they are for the town's end, to beg during life" (5.3.35–38). The best Hal gets in battle from his fat friend is a bottle of sack for a pistol, counterfeit death in the face of an adversary, and spurious claims of heroism against the rebel leader. In the hard glare of political realities the humor again runs dry, as the spectator is forced to question not only Hal's judgment but the king's, as well, for allowing his son the authority to make such an appointment. In part 2 Falstaff's fortunes have suffered little from his manifest dishonesty. His bribery in misusing the king's press is even more blatant; and he assumes, when he hears of King Henry's death, that "the laws of England are at my commandment" (5.3.136–37). Hal's continued amiable association with the rogue when in the company of Nell Quickly and Doll Tearsheet (2.4)—like his earlier willingness to grace the lie of Falstaff's slaying Hotspur in battle and his "discretionary" cowardice in feigning death—lends a kind of unspoken sanction to the increasingly decadent and unlawful behavior; and, in light of his pledge of reconciliation with his father in part 1, his remark, "I feel me much to blame / So idly to profane the precious time" (2.4.361–62), is simply unconvincing, a return to the rationalization of earlier moments.

For one viewing the play from a realistic ideological perspective, all such incidents contribute to a highly negative image of the Lancastrian monarchy. In two additional instances Shakespeare augments his source material to sharpen this attitude. At Gaultree Forest, for example, Holinshed records that the earl of Westmoreland employs trickery to overcome Mowbray and the archbishop of York, leaders of the rebel forces:

When the earle of Westmerland perceiued the forces of the aduersaries, . . . he subtillie deuised how to quaile their purpose. . . . [W]hen they were met with like number on either part, the articles were read ouer, and without anie more adoo, the earle of Westmerland and those that were with him agreed to doo their best, to see that a reformation might be had, according to the same. The earle of Westmerland vsing more policie than the rest: "Well (said he) then our trauell is come to the wished end: and where our people haue been long in armour, let them depart home to their woonted trades and occupations; in the meane time let vs drinke togither in signe of agreement, that the people on both sides maie see it, and know that it is true, that we be light at a point." . . . [B]ut in the meane time, whilst the people of the archbishops side withdrew awaie, the number of the contrarie part increased, according to order giuen by the earle of Westmerland; and yet the archbishop perceiued not that he was deceiued, vntill the earle of Westmerland arrested both him and the earl marshall with diuerse other. (3:37–38)

By transferring Westmoreland's role to Prince John of Lancaster, Shakespeare directly implicates the royal family in this "shameful perfidy,"[21] and he darkens the moral implications through John's swearing "by the honor of my blood" that the enemies' "griefs shall be with speed redress'd" if they will "[d]ischarge [their] powers unto their several counties, / As we will ours" (pt. 2, 4.2.55, 59, 61–62); when the trap has been sprung and the leaders arrested and sentenced to "the block of death, / Treason's true bed," John audaciously quips that "God, and not we, hath safely fought to-day" (122–23, 121).

The second incident, admittedly more minor is nonetheless significant in revealing the extent to which Hal, like his father and brother, is consummately political in his sublimation of sentiment and emotion to public image. Holinshed reports, of the reprobate friends of Hal's youth, that although the new king banished them ten miles from the court they were "not vnrewarded, or else vnpreferred" (3:61). In Shakespeare, on the other hand, John's observation that Henry's "wonted followers / Shall all be very well provided for" is directly contradicted by the Chief Justice's orders that Falstaff and "all his company" shall be taken directly "to the Fleet" (pt. 2, 5.5.98–99, 92, 91). Considering earlier instances of Lancastrian duplicity, Shakespeare's small addition of the prison is grimly ominous. The reference to Bardolph in *Henry V* is similar; when Henry is informed that his previous acquaintance has been arrested in France and sentenced to death for stealing a pax, he proclaims, apparently utterly without emotion, "We would have all such offenders so cut off" (3.6.107–8). Here he sacrifices his friend without hesitation to the "managed insecurity" upon which obedience is constructed.

While *Richard II* focuses ideologically on the extension of monarchical power over the nobility, and *1,2 Henry IV*, on methods of legitimation for questionable authority, *Henry V* is concerned primarily with the processes of the display of power, specifically monarchic power in the service of martial imperialism. If the *Henry IV* plays are training grounds for Prince Hal, they have produced a leader of 'steely determination with a personality unfettered by the normal boundaries of moral and emotional circumspection but also one who with crafty psychological suasion succeeds in convincing subjects of all classes that he acts in the best interest of England's national destiny. This brilliant king of history and legend moves through Shakespeare's lines as a conquering hero subject to seemingly endless adulation. And this vision has been at the center of much traditional criticism. Henry, for example, is "the copybook paragon of kingly virtue,"[22] conceived *"con-amore"* by the playwright,[23] a supreme leader,[24] a "synthesizing Elizabethan genius,"[25] a "Machiavel of goodness."[26] Yet there have long been critics simply unable to abide this figure. For them he is an "amiable monster"[27] possessed of "gross vices,"[28] a "murderer"[29] fit only "for whatever is animal in human affairs,"[30] a Hotspur without charm,[31] his father's true son,[32] a "dead man walking,"[33] a consummate Machiavel.[34]

Such polarized critical evaluations indirectly reflect the thesis of this study—that essentially the same kind of diversity of response occurred among the contemporary spectators of this and most other chronicle plays and that it happened by authorial design. The theater, playwrights, and players, as Louis Montrose writes, "exemplify the contradictions of Elizabethan society and make these contradictions their subject."[35] Whether covertly the motivation was a seditiously antimonarchical attack upon Tudor absolutism, at one extreme, or merely a pragmatic effort to create dramatic entertainment with reasonably good chances for success with a diversified Elizabethan audience, at the other—or whether the concept of history was by now consonant with ideological confrontation—obviously varied to some degree from one playwright to another, but consistently, these plays do build in their own internal dialectic. And none does so more extensively than *Henry V*,[36] the culmination for Shakespeare of a decade of interest in both English and Roman history.

Enmeshed with the brassy patriotism of the play, for those spectators interested in seeing it, are calculated devices by which governmental power establishes and maintains itself. For one thing, Henry is careful to avoid the least appearance of warmongering. In the final lines of *2 Henry IV* Prince John of Lancaster prophesies that war with France is likely: "I heard a bird so sing, / Whose music, to my thinking, pleas'd the King" (5.5.107–8). Yet, instead of publicly initiating such a policy in *Henry V*, Henry is the master calculator, able to conceal his own thirst for expansion and military glory in the seeming tolerance of the vested interests of those around him. Fearful of a bill pending in parliament that would strip from the church fully half of the secular lands in its possession, and doubtless aware of the king's martial desires, the archbishop of Canterbury has made an offer "As touching France, to give a greater sum / Than ever at one time the clergy yet / Did to his predecessors part withal" (1.1.79–81). This offer, a bribe by any other name, comes with full exposition of the "severals and unhidden passages" (86) concerning his genealogical right to the French crown. The situation, in other words, is orchestrated to give the appearance of an outpouring of public support for war, and Henry even has the luxury of being able to appear prudently cautious, urging the clergy to proceed "justly and religiously" (1.2.10); in doing so, he three times within eleven lines invokes God's name (13, 18, 23), thus effectively appropriating "religious metaphysic in the legitimation of war."[37] The illogicality of arguing on the one hand that the Salique law (which denies succession through the female) does not apply to the land of France and thus cannot be used to bar Henry's claim (36–55) and, on the other, that the French claim to the throne is "crooked," in part because it descends through woman (64–95), seems to bother no one; obviously the important logic is that the private interest of both sides is being served.

Once religion has publicly become the ally of Henry's martial cause, he invokes it no fewer than sixty times throughout the play. For instance, he concludes his consultation with the priests with the comment, "[B]y God's help / And yours, the noble sinews of our power, . . . we'll bend [France] to our awe, / Or break it all to pieces" (222–25). On the eve of Agincourt he admonishes Bedford, in the name of "God Almighty" (4.1.3), to find sufficient courage for the impending danger. At the onset of the battle Salisbury declares, "God's arm [will] strike with us," and Henry's speech is peppered with "God's will," "Good God," "God, dispose the day" (4.3.5, 23, 92, 133). And the success against overwhelming odds provokes "O God, thy arm was here, . . . Take it, God, / For it is none but thine, . . . [Let us not] take that praise from God / Which is his only, . . . God fought for us" (4.8.106, 111–12, 115–16, 120). The church, in a word, offers God as a rallying cry for a war that, not insignificantly, greatly expands Henry's wealth and empire; and the king is careful to exploit that support at stress points where appropriation of the deity is needed to assure unquestioned support and obedience.

Such obedience is also reinforced through the conscious process of transforming the enemy into the alien or "other," a propagandistic device used earlier by Henry IV. Both sides, not surprisingly, utilize this strategy. Henry's grandly patriotic call to his troops to breach the wall at Harfleur, for example, is built on insinuations of genetic exclusion. These "[noblest] English" (3.1.17) bred from "fathers of war-proof" (18) are challenged not to "[d]ishonor" their mothers (22), to "attest / That those whom you call'd fathers did beget" them (22–23), to be a "copy to [men] of grosser blood" (24), to reveal they possess the "mettle of [their] pasture" (27) and are "worth [their] breeding" (28). Likewise, at Agincourt Henry declares that he "would not die in that man's company" (4.3.38) who fears to fight the odds of France; "we happy few" he designates a "band of brothers" who render "accurs'd" those remaining abed in England (60, 65). For the opposing army, to the contrary, English are "bastard Normans" from that nook-shotten isle of Albion" (3.5.10, 14); the English king is "wretched and peevish" (3.7.132), his followers "fat-brain'd" (133) and without "intellectual armor" (138); they are "mastiffs" (141), "[f]oolish curs" (143) with "only stomachs to eat and none to fight" (152–53).

Obedience is reinforced, as well, by raising the level of anxiety through intimidation, both verbal and physical. Henry will "strike the Dolphin blind" (1.2.280), turning tennis "balls to gun-stones" (282) that will make "many a thousand widows . . . [m]ock mothers from their sons" (284, 286). Those "poor souls" (2.4.104) who dare to resist will be consumed by "hungry war" (104) with its "vasty jaws" (105), and the land will be filled with "widows' tears," "orphans' cries," "dead men's blood," and "privy maidens' groans" (106, 107). Those in Harfleur Henry threatens to bury in ashes (3.3.9); he will unleash "enraged soldiers" (25) to "hot and forcing violation" (21) that will mow "fresh virgins" and "flow'ring infants" (14) like grass:

> look to see
> The blind and bloody soldier with foul hand
> [Defile[the locks of your shrill-shriking daughters;
> Your fathers taken by the silver beards,
> And their most reverend heads dash'd to the walls;
> Your naked infants spitted upon pikes. . . .
>
> (33–38)

According to Holinshed, Henry, although agreeing to "certaine conditions" of mercy should the inhabitants yield the city, nonetheless proceeded to sack the town, "to the great gain of the Englishmen . . . [and] the distresse whereto the people . . . were driuen" (3:73–74). Various critics point to Shakespeare's more humane ruler in his pledge that he will "use mercy to them all" (3.3.54), but the French king's later comment that Henry "sweeps through our land / With pennons painted in the blood of Harflew" (3.5.48–49) suggests the possibility of another example of politic Lancastrian oath breaking. Certainly there is no question about the physical violence in the public execution of Cambridge, Grey, and Scroop for high treason at Southampton (2.2), of Bardolph's hanging (3.6), or of the slaughter of the French prisoners (4.6). Each incident in its own way through fear and wonder "blocks the anger and resentment that would well up against what must, if contemplated in a secure state, seem an unjust order."[38]

One final example: the play demonstrates the quintessential patriarchal use of political marriage to gain some assurance of dynastic longevity beyond the present generation. Despite Henry's protestation, "By mine honor, in true English, I love thee, Kate" (5.2.220–21), there is little emotion and even less passion in his scheme. When the princess is offered with a dowry of "petty and unprofitable dukedoms" (chorus 3.31), he flatly rejects her and proceeds with his invasion. Only when she will secure the entire kingdom does she become his "capital demand, compris'd / Within the fore-rank of our articles" (5.2.96–97). Clearly for him she now represents the nation ("[I]n loving me, you should love the friend of France; for I love France so well, that I will not part with a village of it; I will have it all mine" [172–75]) and the opportunity for an heir to retain it ("Shall not thou and I . . . compound a boy, half French, half English . . . ? [206–8]").

If the play reflects the various strategies for exploiting authority, it also depicts the soft underside of society that such strategies are intended to contain. Nym, for instance, "dare[s] not fight; but . . . will wink and hold out [his] iron." "I will live so long as I may" (2.1.7–8, 14). He, Pistol, and Bardolph, as "sworn brothers to France" (12–13), go not with the fire of patriotism in their eyes but like "horse-leeches, my boys, / To suck, to suck, the very blood to suck!" (2.3.55–56). Once there, they "will steal any thing, and call it purchase" (3.2.41–42); now "sworn brothers in filching" (44–45), they are described by their boy as three "antics [who] do not amount to a man" (31–32). The fruit of Bardolph's labor I have already remarked upon; Nym receives the same sentence (4.4.72–73), and Pistol, after having been beaten and disgraced by Fluellen, swears to return to England and turn cutpurse: "And patches will I get unto these cudgell'd scars, / And [swear] I got them in the Gallia wars" (5.1.88–89). For another example, the assumption that Henry unites all English nationalities against a common foe is depicted in the play itself (3.2) as nothing more than factious quarreling that only the king's express prohibition holds within reasonable check. As Anthony S. Brennan observes, "The squabbling of the national representatives is a comic reduction of those factional struggles"[39] that have plagued England even to this day. For yet another, in disguise as Harry le Roy, the king is forced to hear his cause questioned (4.1.129–87) and his sworn vow never to desert his men (and be saved by ransom) refuted (121–23). When the common soldier Williams challenges him to fight, Henry embraces an argument that, later, his social position will not allow him to honor (another example, albeit minor, of Lancastrian oath breaking).[40] Such incidents tend to erode the common ground of acceptable behavior between king and subject and to reveal more clearly the methods by which authority and control operate.

Perhaps the single most significant feature responsible for provoking diametrically opposite critical reactions to *Henry V* is Shakespeare's use of what might best be termed mirror scenes, in that they reflect images in reverse. The effect, somewhat like a mental strobe light, tends to freeze the moment and forces the spectator to see an action from more than a single angle. Consider, for example, the hyperbolic rhetoric of the prologue, with references to the stage's inability to contain the struggles of two mighty monarchies suddenly transformed into the almost sleazy, back-room atmosphere in which a few figures huddle together to protect material self-interests (1.1). Or consider the king's rousing call to dazzle France with his "well-hallow'd cause" (1.2.293), namely his right to the throne of France, juxtaposed to the scene of the rebels at Southampton, who—at least the better informed in the audience would realize—acted "to exalt to the crowne" the son of Edward III's oldest surviving line, "Edmund earle of March as heir to Lionell duke of Clarence" (Holinshed 3:71);[41] in effect, the same logic that genealogically would gain Henry the throne of France would lose him the throne of England. Or, consider the irony in Henry's imperialistic venture (a kind of robbery at the national level) contrasted with Pistol's declaration of robbery at the personal level (2.4); the irony in Henry's heroic stature as he accepts money from the church for his war chest (some certainly would consider it a bribe or a kind of robbery) compared with Bardolph's villainous stature as he is executed for robbing the church (3.6),[42]; the irony in Henry's new image as caring friend to England even as his erstwhile companion lies dying and abandoned (2.1, 2.4)—a point reinforced later in Fluellen's attempt to justify Falstaff's "turn[ing] away" by citing the classical analogy of Alexander's killing his friend Cleitus (4.7). Henry's stirring challenge, "Once more unto the breach, dear friends" (3.1.1), is followed directly by Bardolph's " On, on, on, on, on! To the breach, to the breach!" (3.2.1–2); if in one scene safety is freely abandoned to cause, the other yields nothing but Nym's rejoinder to "stay. The knocks are too hot" (3–4) and the boy's retort that he "would give all [his] fame for a pot of ale and safety" (13). Similarly, Henry's inspirational charge to his troops to fight like true heroes at Agincourt (4.3) is juxtaposed to the treasonous Pistol taking a bribe for the release of his French prisoner (4.4). The same principle is at work in pairing the comments about Henry in disguise giving cheer and comfort to all around him (chorus, act 4) with what he actually encounters in the distinctly antimonarchic comments of Bates and Williams (4.1) that subject "the heroic vision of Henry and his army to an intensive interrogation."[43]

Obviously this structural complementarity is far too frequent to be coincidental. Here Shakespeare utilizes what Richard Levin has called a spatial integration of plots to create, through ambivalencies and ironical tensions, a foil to Henry's glorious exploits. The effect, as Levin observes, is that of a "musical chord, contingent upon the absolute emotional 'pitch' of each action as well as the relative emotional 'distance' between them."[44] The task of interrelating the components of the plot to achieve this response, however, is left essentially to the spectators. They alone are privy to Canterbury's and Ely's desire to protect a large portion of the church's wealth; they alone must relate the nature of Nym's, Bardolph's, and Pistol's military activities to the stylized heroism of the English army and its idealized leader. The references to Falstaff's reaction to his repudiation and the momentary pathos during Nell Quickly's description of his death are never explored diretly in relation to Henry. Any soul-searching evidenced in the king's soliloquy in the middle of the play, except in the mind of the viewer, has evaporated in the Henry of act 5. The chorus, instead of providing an integrating and analytic commentary, delivers a veritable encomium on the magnificent and heroic English military accomplishments.

In a word, the spectators are forced to relate the various components of the play; in doing so, they must provide, and test the limitations of, the political values by which to respond to the decisions and actions that precipitate Henry's mounting successes. For certainly the concerns of the *Henriad* are above all political. By focusing on the strategies of legitimation and exploitation of authority and by constantly juxtaposing the orthodox with the unorthodox, *1,2 Henry IV* and *Henry V* expose the official ideology for what it is, whatever one's affiliation—"an illusion effectively used as an instrument of power."[45]

Conclusion

Since what clearly emerges from a structural and political analysis of the English chronicle plays is that they were constructed to appeal to a wide diversity of spectators, it would be reductionistic to argue that they exclusively advocate any specific ideology. What is clear is that they are "problematically multivocal."[1] While it is highly unlikely that such drama comprised a "fully deliberate and conscious arrangement," an "implicit social contract between authors and authorities," as Annabel Patterson has claimed,[2] the playwrights, in order to succeed, were forced to develop dramatic strategies that would interact inherently with the various social strata in the audience, forging a "language and a means of representation that would satisfy a heterogeneous audience representing diverse *loci* of power and support."[3] The queen and her court circle, the London authorities with their puritanical readiness to censor anything overtly seditious or decadent—both had to be considered if the play was to have a chance of finding its way to the stage. But, once there, the action had to hold the attention of a broad public drawn at least in part from the artisan and working classes. "Allowing a stoole as well to the Farmers sonne as to your Templar," tobacco-"stinkard," "sweet Courtier," "car-man," and "tinker,"[4] the Elizabethan theater was subject to market forces that rendered it especially vulnerable to the influence of subordinate and emergent classes.[5] While the playwright was not free to create onstage an arrant subversion of authority (and perhaps had no desire to do so), what he could do and did was to develop strategies to explore critically the sources of authority, in terms of both its social divisions and its manifestations regarding a monarch's personal life. The rupture between the rhetoric of cere-mony or authority and the actuality of its deeds is exploited to reveal a hollowness at the center without overtly portraying social dissension.

Equally important, plays like *The Famous Victories of Henry V, Edward III, Edmund Ironside, Sir John Oldcastle, Thomas, Lord Cromwell, 1,2,3 Henry VI, King John, Richard I, 1, 2 Henry IV,* and *Henry V* form part of a general movement toward what amounts

129

to a new mode of historical inquiry. This new historiography, which developed in British intellectual life between 1580 and 1640,[6] moves beyond Ciceronian platitudes about history's moral utility, beyond the services of didacticism through a reflection of a providential view of human events, beyond history as a response to the tide of patriotism surrounding the defeat of the Armada, beyond history as a tool of the Tudor establishment. Individuals began to look beyond medieval providentialism, to view national problems "in a relation to the coordinates of time and place which is as familiar to the modern mind as it would have been strange to the medieval."[7] Spurred by the search for precedents in English common law and by Protestant theologians who sought causes, motivations, and consequences in pre-Reformation England, by advances in philology that opened up a new knowledge of Anglo-Saxon history, the learned world by the end of the sixteenth century "was becoming habituated to critical arguments founded on records and historical precedents."[8] On the one hand, more adequate facilities for research became available while, on the other, the invention of new instruments made possible advances in precision in virtually all fields.[9] "Across subjects ranging from physical cosmology at one extreme to theology and social history at the other,"[10] the late Tudor society was characterized by a greater degree of historical consciousness.

Dealing with the themes and passions of political power, the history plays of the 1580s and the 1590s contributed directly to this new mentality, depicting a "transition from a medieval period understood to be stable, providentially protected and decorously chivalric[,] to a world of crude *Realpolitik*."[11] Subject to widely varying, virtually diametrically opposite interpretations, such plays embody their own internal dialectic. Through this multiplicity of perspective, they begin to incorporate a view of history as a process of change, as self-determined, as a struggle between aristocratic houses and the monarchic state, between military and civilian interests, as a conflict regarding matters of succession and inheritance—to view history as founded in ideological confrontation.

"Reinstalled in their historical context,"[12] such chronicle plays refuse to be bound by a particular design or ideology. They are as rich and ultimately as contradictory as the motivations that generate human action; for precisely this reason they fulfill the complex demands of their contemporary public-stage audiences. In the final analysis, they offer little definitive guidance or shaping of events in such a manner as to delimit the meaning or significance of history, and the spectator is forced individually to come to terms with the welter of contradictions and conflicting ironies. He may leave the theater assuming that the playwright has depicted the canker at the very heart of monarchical government and hierarchical society, convinced that the play encodes an attack upon the Tudor establishment to which the general public would be attuned. He may, on the other hand, be convinced that the play is not an attack upon monarchism itself, but on its delusions of unlimited power, that the struggle between the king and his subjects effectively denigrates the excessive ambitions of both ruler and aristocracy. He may believe that the play above all exhibits the grave dangers of depraved leadership, or of political division, or of civil dissension, or of nationalistic imperialism run wild. He may believe, on the other hand, that the play affirms England's greatness, or that it suggests potential glory limited only by the degree to which rulers fail to bridle their obsessions and subjects fail to share a monolithic political vision. He may, of course, leave the theater in a muddle, confused at his inability to bring consistent moral values to bear upon a political circle in which "there's none so good, but someone doth him hate" (*Cromwell* 5.4.25). The rare spectator might well leave the theater with precisely that conviction but without the confusion, envisioning the play dispassionately as an artistic assertion of new historiography and a refusal to reduce to simplistic absolutes the complex ambiguities and the human frailties—and the human corruption—inherent in any political process.

Whatever the individual perception, the anonymous histories—along with those of Shakespeare more familiar to our own age—stand as evidence that the chronicle play could appeal to some in its contemporary audiences as a ratification of monarchism and the privileges of class and to others as an instrument of criticism and agitation. The text of such plays, with its varied range of social responses, is itself a form of history as process,[13] shaping the events of the past into a pattern that provided for the lower and middle classes a sense of temporary social release within a framework which the aristocracy would construe, at best, as a panegyric for monarchism or, at worst, as nothing seriously in violation of the constraints of orthodox politics.

Notes

Introduction

1. Alfred Harbage and Samuel Schoenbaum, *Annals of English Drama*, 2d ed., rev. (Philadelphia: University of Pennsylvania Press, 1964), 50–92.

2. Felix E. Schelling, *Elizabethan Drama* (Boston: Houghton Mifflin, 1908), 1:251.

3. Samuel Taylor Coleridge, *The Literary Remains of Samuel Taylor Coleridge*, ed. Henry Nelson Coleridge (London: Pickering, 1836), 2:165.

4. Henry Buckley Charlton, *Shakespeare, Politics and Politicians*, English Association Pamphlet 72 (Oxford: Oxford University Press, 1929), 8.

5. August Wilhelm von Schlegel, *Lectures on Dramatic Art and Literature*, 2d ed., rev., trans. John Black (London: G. Bell, 1889), 419.

6. Lily B. Campbell, *Shakespeare's "Histories"* (San Marino, Calif.: Huntington Library Press, 1947), 15.

7. John Arthur Ransome Marriott, *English History in Shakespeare* (London: Chapman and Hall, 1918), 25.

8. E. M. W. Tillyard, *Shakespeare's History Plays* (New York: Macmillan, 1944), 119.

9. Alfred Harbage, *Shakespeare's Audience* (New York: Columbia University Press, 1941), 90.

10. Robert Weimann, *Shakespeare and the Popular Tradition in the Theater*, ed. Robert Schwartz (Baltimore: Johns Hopkins University Press, 1978), 170.

11. Ann Jennalie Cook, *The Privileged Playgoers of Shakespeare's London, 1576–1640* (Princeton: Princeton University Press, 1981), 272.

12. Stephen Booth, review of *The Privileged Playgoers of Shakespeare's London, 1576–1640*, by Ann Jennalie Cook, *Medieval and Renaissance Drama in England* 2 (1985): 309–10.

13. Martin Butler, *Theater in Crisis, 1632–1643* (Cambridge: Cambridge University Press, 1970), 301.

14. Andrew Gurr, *Playgoing in Shakespeare's London* (Cambridge: Cambridge University Press, 1987), 140.

15. From a sermon delivered in 1577, cited by Edmund K. Chambers, *The Elizabethan Stage*, 4 vols. (Oxford: Oxford University Press, Clarendon Press, 1923), 4:197.

16. Simon Shepherd, *Marlowe and the Politics of Elizabethan Theatre* (New York: St. Martin's Press, 1986), xiv. Henry Crosse observed in 1603 that plays provoked spectators to "execrable actions, commotions, mutinies, rebellions" (sig. Q_1); another wrote in 1597 that the theaters provided a meeting place for "contrivers of treason and other idele and daungerous persons," citing especially the "mutinous attempts" of apprentices and servants ("Dramatic Records of the City

of London: The Remembrancia," *Malone Society Collections*, vol. 1, pt. 1, ed. Edmund K. Chambers and Walter Wilson Greg (1980), 80, 76).

17. Steven Mullaney, *The Place of the Stage: License, Play, and Power in Renaissance England* (Chicago: University of Chicago Press, 1988), vii.

18. Michel Foucault, *Discipline and Punish: The Birth of the Prison*, trans. A. Sheridan (New York: Pantheon, 1977), 189.

19. Steven Mullaney, "Brothers and Others, or the Art of Alienation," in *Cannibals, Witches, and Divorce: Estranging the Renaissance*, ed. Marjorie Garber (Baltimore: Johns Hopkins University Press, 1987), 87.

20. Paul N. Siegel, *Shakespeare's English and Roman History Plays* (Rutherford, N.J.: Fairleigh Dickinson University Press, 1986), 16.

21. David Michael Palliser, *The Age of Elizabeth: England Under the Later Tudors 1547–1603* (London: Longman, 1983), 301.

22. Ernest W. Talbert, *The Problem of Order* (Chapel Hill: University of North Carolina Press, 1962), 121.

23. Walter P. Hall and Robert G. Albion, *A History of England and the British Empire* (Boston: Ginn, 1946), 302.

24. Lawrence Stone, *The Crisis of the Aristocracy 1558–1641* (Oxford: Oxford University Press, Clarendon Press, 1965), 7; see also R. B. Outhwaite, *Inflation in Tudor and Early Stuart England* (London: Macmillan, 1969).

25. J. E. Christopher Hill, *Reformation to Industrial Revolution: A Social and Economic History of Britain, 1530–1780* (New York: Random House, 1967), 31–32.

26. Lawrence Stone, *The Family, Sex and Marriage in England, 1500–1800* (New York: Harper and Row, 1977), 7.

27. Robin Wells, *Shakespeare, Politics and the State* (London: Macmillan, 1986), 139.

28. Terry Eagleton, *William Shakespeare* (Oxford: Blackwell, 1986), 104.

29. Palliser, *Age of Elizabeth*, 309.

30. Malcolm Evans, *Signifying Nothing: Truth's True Contents in Shakespeare's Text* (Athens: University of Georgia Press, 1986), 34.

31. Michael D. Bristol, *Carnival and Theater: Plebeian Culture and the Structure of Authority in Renaissance England* (London: Methuen, 1985), 36.

32. Richard V. Lindabury, *A Study of Patriotism in the Elizabethan Drama* (Princeton: Princeton University Press, 1931), 200.

33. Among recent studies, for example, see Jonathan Dollimore and Alan Sinfield, eds., *Political Shakespeare* (Ithaca: Cornell University Press, 1985); Jonathan Goldberg, *James I and the Politics of Literature* (Baltimore: Johns Hopkins University Press, 1984); Annabel Patterson, *Censorship and Interpretation: The Conditions of Reading and Writing in Early Modern England* (Madison: University of Wisconsin Press, 1984); Leonard Tennenhouse, *Power on Display: The Politics of Shakespeare's Genres* (London: Methuen, 1986); Graham Holderness, Nick Potter, and John Turner, *Shakespeare: The Play of History* (Iowa City: University of Iowa Press, 1987); Jean Howard and Marion O'Connor, eds., *Shakespeare Reproduced: The Text in History and Ideology* (London: Methuen, 1988); Stephen Greenblatt, *Shakespearean Negotiations: The Circulation of Social Energy in Renaissance England* (Berkeley: University of California Press, 1988).

34. Julia Briggs, *This Stage-Play World* (Oxford: Oxford University Press, 1983), 162.

Chapter 1. *The Famous Victories of Henry V*

1. 1574—Bernard M. Ward, *"The Famous Victories of Henry V:* Its Place in Elizabethan Dramatic Literature," *Review of English Studies* 4 (1928): 281; 1583–88—Harbage and Schoenbaum, *Annals of English Drama,* 50; Schelling, *Elizabethan Drama,* 1:257; anterior to Shakespeare's work—Frank Percy Wilson, *Marlowe and the Early Shakespeare* (Oxford: Oxford University Press, Clarendon Press, 1953), 106; "before blank verse had become naturalised on the popular stage"—Wilheim Creizenach, *The English Drama in the Age of Shakespeare* (London: Sidgwick and Jackson, 1926), 28.

2. Seymour M. Pitcher, *The Case for Shakespeare's Authorship of "The Famous Victories of Henry V"* (Albany: State University of New York, 1961), 5.

3. Felix E. Schelling, *Elizabethan Playwrights* (New York: Harper, 1925), 109. A "piece of uncouth but honest old English upholstery" (John Addington Symonds, *Shakespeare's Predecessors in the English Drama* [London: Smith, Elder, 1884], 378), it is one of the most interesting of the pre-Shakespearean history plays (Hugh M. Richmond, *Shakespeare's Political Plays* [New York: Random House, 1967], 8), "for the time of its composition not crude at all" (C. A. Greer, "A Lost Play the Source of Shakespeare's *Henry IV* and *Henry V," Notes and Queries,* n.s., 1 [1954]: 54).

4. Irving Ribner, *The English History Play in the Age of Shakespeare* (Princeton: Princeton University Press, 1957), 69.

5. Madeleine Doran, *Endeavors of Art: A Study of Form in Elizabethan Drama* (Madison: University of Wisconsin Press, 1954), 295.

6. Wilson, *Marlowe,* 106. Edward Capell described it as "a medley of nonsense and ribaldry" (cited in Pitcher, *The Case,* 5); "dry and summary" (Creizenach, *English Drama,* 29), its only claim on our patience is its influence on Shakespeare (C. F. Tucker Brooke, *The Tudor Drama* [Boston: Houghton Mifflin, 1911], 307).

7. Brooke, "The Renaissance (1500–1660)," in *A Literary History of England,* ed. A. C. Baugh (New York: Appleton-Century-Crofts, 1948), 458; Ifor Evans, *A Short History of English Drama* (Harmondsworth, England: Penguin, 1940), 32.

8. Chambers, *The Elizabethan Stage,* 4:17; Harbage and Schoenbaum, *Annals of English Drama,* 50–51.

9. Frederick Gard Fleay, *A Biographical Chronicle of the English Drama, 1559–1642* (London: Reeves and Turner, 1891), 67. See also Brooke, *Tudor,* 307 and Schelling, *Drama,* 1:188.

10. H. Dugdale Sykes, *The Authorship of "The Taming of a Shrew," "The Famous Victories of Henry V," and the Additions to Marlowe's "Faustus,"* Shakespeare Association Paper, 28 February 1919 (London: De La More Press, 1919), 34–35.

11. Ward, *"The Famous Victories,"* 287.

12. Tillyard, *Shakespeare's History Plays,* 174; Pitcher, *"The Famous Victories,"* 6.

13. Doran, *Endeavors of Art,* 114.

14. Schelling, *Drama,* 1:xxviii.

15. Ribner, *English History Play,* 76.

16. Willard Farnham, *The Medieval Heritage of Elizabethan Tragedy* (Oxford: Blackwell, 1936).

17. Lindabury, *A Study of Patriotism,* 48.

18. Brooke, *Tudor,* 331.

19. Ibid., 320.

20. Stephen Greenblatt, "Invisible Bullets: Renaissance Authority and Its

Subversion, *Henry IV* and *Henry V*," in *Political Shakespeare*, ed. Jonathan Dollimore and Alan Sinfield (Ithaca: Cornell University Press, 1985), 42.

21. References are to line numbers in *The Famous Victories of Henry V* in *Chief Pre-Shakespearean Dramas*, ed. Joseph Quincy Adams (Boston: Houghton Mifflin, 1924), 667–90. All additional references are cited parenthetically in the text.

22. Moody E. Prior, *The Drama of Power* (Evanston, Ill.: Northwestern University Press, 1973), 321.

23. Ibid., 345. Both Creizenach (*English Drama*, 29) and Pitcher ("*The Famous Victories*," 93) also admit that Hal's character in the first half reflects not the least hint of potential for such reform.

24. Ribner, *English History Play* 69.

25. Even in this small touch Hal is presumably caught in a lie by the perceptive spectator. While an earlier stage direction specifically indicates that Henry IV weeps, there is no such stage direction for any tears from Hal.

26. Raphael Holinshed, *Holinshed's Chronicles of England, Scotland, and Ireland*, 6 vols. (London: Johnson, 1808), 3:53. All additional references are cited parenthetically in the text.

27. Brooke, *Tudor*, 307.

28. Graham Holderness, *Shakespeare's History* (Dublin: Gill and Macmillan, 1986), 34.

29. Conventional criticism typically transforms such a scene to courtly and aristocratic compliment by focusing on the bumbling constables, "foolish by tradition," who ineptly attempt to mimic their betters in both speech and action (Muriel C. Bradbrook, *The Growth and Structure of Elizabethan Comedy* [London: Chatto and Windus, 1955], 89).

30. There is simply no textual evidence to support Robert Ornstein's earlier claim for Hal's deep grief in the presence of his father (*A Kingdom for a Stage* [Cambridge: Harvard University Press, 1972], 164). Similarly, his incredible comment that the prince here turns away his companions "with a sigh" (169) forces one to wonder just how carefully he read the play.

31. Jonathan Dollimore and Alan Sinfield, "History and Ideology: The Instance of *Henry V*," in *Alternative Shakespeares*, ed. John Drakakis (London: Methuen, 1985), 215.

32. Shakespeare, of course, transfers this incident to the Boar's Head in Eastcheap; Falstaff forces Bardolph and Peto to tickle their noses with speargrass so as, by bloodying their garments, to support his allegation that they fought long and hard against those who counterrobbed them.

33. Niccolo Machiavelli, *Discourses*, trans. Christian Detmold (New York: Random House, 1950), 147.

34. Leonard Tennenhouse, "Strategies of State and Political Plays: *A Midsummer Night's Dream, Henry V, Henry VIII*," in *Political Shakespeare*, ed. Jonathan Dollimore and Alan Sinfield (Ithaca: Cornell University Press, 1985), 120.

Chapter 2. *The Reign of Edward III*

1. John S. Lewis, "The Rash Oath in *Edward III*," *Allegorica* 1 (1976): 269.

2. Tillyard, *Shakespeare's History Plays*, 131.

3. Inna Koskennieme, "Themes and Imagery in *Edward III*," *Neophilologische Mitteilungen* 65 (1964): 446.

4. Karl Wentersdorf, "The Date of *Edward III*," *Shakespeare Quarterly* 16

(1965): 227–31; Frank O'Connor, *The Road to Stratford* (London: Methuen, 1948); Alfred Hart, *Shakespeare and the Homilies* (Melbourne: Melbourne University Press, 1934); Mary Bell, M.A. thesis, University of Liverpool, 1959.

5. Kenneth Muir, "A Reconstruction of *Edward III*," *Shakespeare Survey* 6 (1953): 39–47; William Kozlenko, *Disputed Plays of Shakespeare* (New York: Hawthorne Books, 1974); Edmund K. Chambers, *William Shakespeare: Facts and Problems*, 2 vols. (Oxford: Oxford University Press, Clarendon Press, 1930); Adolphus William Ward, *A History of English Dramatic Literature to the Death of Queen Anne*, 2 vols. (London: Macmillan, 1875); Marco Mincoff, review of *Shakespeare as Collaborator*, by Kennth Muir, *English Studies*, 43 (1963): 216–18; Clifford Leech, Review of *Shakespeare as Collaborator*, by Kenneth Muir, *Notes and Queries*, N.S. 8 (1961): 156–57.

6. Peele: Brooke, *Tudor;* Kyd: G. Lambrechts, "*Edward III*, Oeuvre de Thomas Kyd," *Études Anglaises* 16 (1963): 160–74.

7. 1588: Wentersdorf, "Date," 231; 1596: Adolphus W. Ward and A. R. Waller, *The Cambridge History of English Literature* (Cambridge: Cambridge University Press, 1933), 5:276. Evaluations of the quality of the play vary as widely as do opinions on the date. "Totally lacking in dramatic coherence" to Brooke (*Tudor*, 331), it is "a finished product" to Symonds (*Shakespeare's Predecessors*, 44), "easily maintaining the literary excellence of the plays on Henry VI in the qualities of spirited dialogue, picturesque phrase, and occasional poetical sentiment" (Felix E. Schelling, *The English Chronicle Play* [1902; New York: Haskell House, 1964], 60). Ward, both in *History* (2:224) and in *Cambridge* (5:273), claims that there is a disjuncture in the plot between the love scenes and the war scenes, the one taken from William Painter's *The Palace of Pleasure* and the other from Raphael Holinshed's *Chronicles*. On the other hand, Robert Metcalf Smith (*Froissart and the English Chronicle Play* [New York: Columbia University Press, 1915], 70) argues that John Froissart's *Chronicles*, which includes both elements of the story and which was translated early in the sixteenth century by John Bourchier, second Lord Berners, was the source of the entire play.

8. Ray Livingstone Armstrong, ed., *The Raigne of King Edward III*, in *Six Plays Related to the Shakespeare Canon*, ed. Ephraim B. Everitt and Ray Livingston Armstrong (Copenhagen: Rosenkilde and Bagger, 1965), 197.

9. Wentersdorf, "Date," 231.

10. Brooke, *Tudor*, 332.

11. C. F. Tucker Brooke, *The Shakespeare Apocrypha* (Oxford: Oxford University Press, Clarendon Press, 1918), xxiii.

12. Schelling, *Drama*, 1:411.

13. Convinced of his right to the crown, Edward must also be perceived as "delivering a worthy French nation from tyranny" (David Bevington, *Tudor Drama and Politics* [Cambridge: Harvard University Press, 1968], 201). Both Tillyard, (*History Plays*, 169) and Lewis ("The Rash Oath," 269) focus more specifically on the carnal lust that poses a deterrent to his effective role, and Lewis notes the popularity of the theme in other plays of the period. See also William Alvin Armstrong, *Elizabeth History Plays* (London: Oxford University Press, 1965), ix.

14. References are to the edition of *The Raigne of Edward III*, in *The Complete Works of Shakespeare*, ed. Herbert Farjeon (New York: Nonesuch Press, 1929). All additional references to act, scene, line are cited parenthetically in the text.

15. Brooke, *Tudor*, 331.

16. Tillyard, *History Plays*, 320.

17. Max Meredith Reese, *The Cease of Majesty* (New York: St. Martin's Press, 1961), 84.

18. Lewis ("The Rash Oath," 271) observes that a pattern of a rash oath followed by a contradictory oath that releases one from the binding power of the first occurs in all three sections of the plot—the Scottish invasion, Edward's succumbing to lust, the war in France—and functions as a unifying element in the play.

19. Wentersdorf argues that this report of the Battle of Sluys is modeled on reports of the English victory over the Spanish Armada in 1588; cannon is not known to have been used until much later than Sluys, and the name of a ship mentioned by the mariner—the *Nonpareil*—was one of Elizabeth's ships in the fight against the Spanish ("Date," 228–30).

Chapter 3. *Sir John Oldcastle*

1. Ludwig Tieck, cited in Brooke, *Apocrypha*, xi; Schlegel, *Lectures on Dramatic Art*, 445.

2. Philip Henslowe, *Henslowe's Diary*, ed Walter Wilson Greg, 2 vols. (London: Bullen, 1904), 1:113.

3. Brooke, *Apocrypha*, xxvii; Schelling, *Drama*, 1:278.

4. George B. Harrison, *Elizabethan Plays and Players* (Ann Arbor: University of Michigan Press, 1956), 202.

5. Alfred Harbage, *Shakespeare and the Rival Traditions* (New York: Macmillan, 1952), 144.

6. Kozlenko, *Disputed Plays*, 328.

7. Ibid., 445.

8. Harbage, *Traditions*, 237.

9. Brooke, *Apocrypha*, xxvii.

10. Kozlenko, *Disputed Plays*, 328.

11. Harrison, *Plays and Players*, 203.

12. Ward, *History of English Dramatic Literature*, 1:434–35; William Hazlitt, *Characters of Shakespeare's Plays* (London: Templeman, 1817), 1:260.

13. Ward, *History of English Dramatic Literature*, 1:434–35.

14. Schelling, *Drama*, 279.

15. An entry marked "as a gefte" in *Henslowe's Diary* indicates that the authors received a bonus when the play reached the stage: "Receved of Mr Hincheloe for Mr Mundaye & the Reste of the poets at the playnge of Sr John oldcastell the ferste tyme" (1:113).

16. References are to *The First Part of Sir John Oldcastle*, in Kozlenko, ed., *Disputed Plays*, 333–68. All additional references to act, scene, line are cited parenthetically in the text.

17. At Scroop's request that Cambridge "make rehearsal / How you do stand entitled to the crown" (3.1.1–2), Cambridge meticulously explains his legal claim to the English throne. The son of Edmund Langley, duke of York, who was the fifth son of Edward III, he has married Anne Mortimer, the great-granddaughter of Lionel, duke of Clarence, the third son. As a direct descendent of the oldest surviving line, Anne has lineal precedence over Henry V, whose father, Henry IV (descended from John of Gaunt, the fourth son), was a "false intruder [who did] usurp the crown" (31). Scroope, Grey, and Chartres (on be-

half of the king of France) solemnly swear to uphold this right and to "set up [Cambridge] and [his] renowned wife" (62). No one can deny the principle of self-interest, especially in the case of Chartres, but the fact remains that law—if not possession—is on their side.

18. If Cobham's unquestioning devotion supports a surface image of an immensely popular young king prepared to rule for the good of his kingdom, this same monarch, in degree if not in kind, is no less responsible than Rochester for Oldcastle's oppression and condemnation.

Chapter 4. *Thomas, Lord Cromwell*

1. Cited in Baldwin Maxwell, *Studies in the Shakespeare Apocrypha* (New York: Columbia University Press, King's Crown Press, 1956), 95.

2. Arthur Frederick Hopkinson, ed., *The Life and Death of Thomas, Lord Cromwell* (London: W. E. Sims, 1891), x.

3. Fleay, *Biographical Chronicle* 1:161.

4. Arthur Acheson, *Shakespeare, Chapman, and Sir Thomas More* (New York: Hackett, 1931), 117.

5. Maxwell, *Studies*, 106–8.

6. August Wilhelm von Schlegel, *Vorlesungen über Dramaturgische Künst und Litteratur*, 2 vols. (Leipzig: Weidman, 1846) 2:308.

7. Algernon Charles Swinburne, *A Study of Shakespeare* (London: Worthington, 1880), 232.

8. The play, for example, is little more than a "lifeless and scamped piece of journeywork" (Symonds, *Shakespeare's Predecessors*, 389), a primitive tragedy (Farnham, *Medieval Heritage*, 387) of loosely strung scenes (Frederick S. Boas, *An Introduction to Tudor Drama* [Oxford: Oxford University Press, Clarendon Press, 1933], 121) "with hardly a passage . . . which excites special attention" (Brooke, *Apocrypha*, xxviii). Others describe it as "a production of merit" (Schelling, *Elizabethan Playwrights*, 215; *Drama*, 1:286), a series of biographical scenes connected by a chorus that "may have produced a considerable effect" (*History of English Dramatic Literature*, 2:234). The subplot is "skillfully woven" into the scenes focusing on Thomas, and the first half of the play, in particular, is "from the pen of an experienced and skillful playmaker" (Maxwell, *Shakespeare Apocrypha*, 75, 82).

9. Robert B. Sharpe, *The Real War of the Theaters* (Boston: Heath, 1935), 194.

10. Ribner, *English History Play*, 205.

11. References are to *The Life and Death of Thomas, Lord Cromwell*, in Kozlenko, *Disputed Plays*, 266–88. All additional references are cited by act, scene, line parenthetically in the text.

12. Symonds, *Shakespeare's Predecessors*, 389.

13. Maxwell, *Shakespeare Apocrypha*, 86.

14. Kozlenko, *Disputed Plays*, 263.

15. Maxwell, *Shakespeare Apocrypha*, 73.

16. Schelling, *Playwrights*, 216.

17. Maxwell observes that there is no such incident in the source for the play (*Shakespeare Apocrypha*, 80). The anonymous playwright has obviously created whole cloth a situation that focuses on the exploitation of the commoner.

18. Bevington, *Tudor Drama and Politics*, 294.

19. Again the playwright has played loose with history. In this particular inci-

dent John Foxe, who makes no mention whatsoever of Gardiner, reports that Cromwell said "he wished his dagger in him that had dissolved this marriage [Henry and Anne of Cleves]" (*The Acts and Monuments of John Foxe*, ed. Stephen Reed Cattley, 8 vols. [London: Seeley and Burnside, 1838] 5:402).

20. The messenger says only that Bedford desired Cromwell to read it because "it doth concern you near" (5.2.9).

21. Ribner, *English History Play*, 218.

Chapter 5. *Edmund Ironside*

1. James O. Halliwell-Phillips, *A Dictionary of Old English Plays* (London: J. R. Smith, 1860), 62.

2. Early in the decade—Frederick S. Boas, *Shakespeare and the Universities* (New York: Appleton, 1923), 111–17; Eleanore Boswell, ed., *Edmund Ironside*, The Malone Society Reprints (Oxford: Oxford University Press, 1928), x; Clifford Leech, "The Two-Part Play: Marlowe and the Early Shakespeare," *Shakespeare Jahrbuch*, 94 (1958): 97; Ernest W. Talbert, *Elizabethan Drama and Shakespeare's Early Plays* (Chapel Hill: University of North Carolina Press, 1963), 176. 1590–1600—Walter Wilson Greg, *Dramatic Documents From the Elizabethan Playhouses* (Oxford: Oxford University Press, Clarendon Press, 1931), 256; Gerald Eades Bentley, *The Jacobean and Caroline Stage* (Oxford: Oxford University Press, Clarendon Press, 1941), 1:581; Ribner, *English History Play*, 242. 1595—Schoenbaum and Harbage, *Annals of English Drama*, 62; Geoffrey Bullough, "Pre-Conquest History Themes in Elizabethan Drama," in *Medieval Literature and Civilisation*, ed. D. A. Pearsall and R. A. Waldron (London: Athlone Press, 1969), 293. Late in the decade—Frank P. Wilson, *Shakespeare and Other Studies* (Oxford: Oxford University Press, 1969), 46; Richard Proudfoot, "*Edmund Ironside*," *Times Literary Supplement*, 22 October 1982, 1162.

3. Eric Sams, *Shakespeare's Lost Play, "Edmund Ironside"* (New York: St. Martins Press, 1985), 39. The early stages of the argument can be followed through comments in the *Times Literary Supplement* by Eric Sams (13 August 1982, 879; 24 September 1982, 1037; 29 October 1982, 119), Robert Fleissner (3 September 1982, 947), Richard Proudfoot (17 September 1982, 1010; 22 October 1982, 1162), Peter Milward (19 November 1982, 1273), MacD. P. Jackson (10 September 1982, 973), Eliot Slater (18 March 1983, 268), and Gary Taylor (1 April 1983, 328).

4. Sams, *Shakespeare's Lost Play*, 26.

5. Ibid., 28.

6. Ibid., 9.

7. Ibid., 1.

8. Ibid., 2.

9. Boas, *Shakespeare*, 111.

10. Boswell, *Edmund Ironside*, xii.

11. M. Hope Dodds, "*Edmund Ironside* and *The Love-sick King*," *Modern Language Review* 19 (1924): 166.

12. Boswell, *Edmund Ironside*, xi.

13. Talbert, *Elizabethan Drama*, 176.

14. Ribner, *English History Play*, xi.

15. Bernard Spivack, *Shakespeare and the Allegory of Evil* (New York: Columbia University Press, 1958), 340.

16. Boas, *Shakespeare*, 113.

17. Ephraim B. Everitt describes it as "history presented without bias," with both kings studious of the principles of good government (*The Young Shakespeare: Studies in Documentary Evidence* [Copenhagen: Rosenkilde and Bagger, 1954], 149, 150).

18. All references are to Sams's edition. Additional references to act, scene, line are cited parenthetically in the text.

19. Curiously, Bullough sees an emphasis on the "arrogance and cruelty of the Danes" ("Pre-Conquest History Themes," 296); and to David Riggs, Canute exists "primarily to elicit and test the hero's special virtues" (*Shakespeare's Heroical Histories: "Henry VI" and Its Literary Tradition* [Cambridge: Harvard University Press, 1971], 60).

20. Dodds, *"Edmund Ironside,"* 160.

21. Bullough's incredible comment that "Edmund is not deceived" ("Pre-Conquest History Themes," 297) forces one to wonder just how closely he read the play.

22. Boas, *Shakespeare*, 40.

23. Spivack, *Shakespeare*, 340.

24. Ibid., 345.

25. David Bevington believes that the play offended the censors because of its specific support for Essex in its "glorification of the military leader who is a friend of the poor and the common soldier" (*Tudor Drama and Politics*, 291). R. B. Sharpe, on the other hand, argues that the issue of a villain's assisting a Danish claimant to the throne indirectly "suggests a reference to James" (*The Real War of the Theaters*, 100).

26. The scene is "unparalleled in Elizabethan drama for its naïve and farcical representation of two church dignitaries" (Everitt, *Young Shakespeare*, 50).

27. Spivack, *Shakespeare*, 373.

28. Talbert, *Elizabethan Drama*, 19.

29. The conflict inherent in selfless altruism and the reality of the political context is most certainly what led Boas to brand as inconsistent Edmund's role as "patriot king" and his "quixotic exuberance after Canute's surrender (*Shakespeare*, 140). The division of the kingdom would be "anathema to every watching Elizabethan" (Ribner, *English History Play*, 243).

30. E. K. Chambers, *William Shakespeare* (Oxford: Oxford University Press, Clarendon Press, 1930), 1:111.

31. Everitt, *Young Shakespeare*, 50.

32. Sams, *Shakespeare's Lost Play*, 21–25.

33. Ribner, for example, suggests that Edricus may have been modeled after *Richard III* (*English History Play*, 242); Proudfoot, that the play "appears to echo *Richard II*" ("*Edmund Ironside*," 1162); Leech, that the structure reflects the influence of *Tamburlaine* ("Two-Part," 90); Everitt, that numerous passages "call up the same poetic and dramatic patterns as appear in the Shakespeare canon" (*Young Shakespeare*, 115).

34. Boas, *Shakespeare*, 141.

35. Arthur Henry Bullen, *A Collection of Old English Plays*, 4 vols. (London: Wyman and Sons, 1882), 1:420.

36. Schelling, *Chronicle Play*, 2–3.

37. Ribner, *English History Play*, 8.

38. Tillyard, *Shakespeare's History Plays*, 17.

39. Riggs, *Shakespeare's Heroical Histories*, 9.

Chapter 6. The *Henry VI* Plays

1. Robert Weimann, "Discourse, Ideology and the Crisis of Authority in Post-Reformation England," *The Yearbook of Research in English and American Literature* 5 (1987): 110.

2. J. E. Christopher Hill, *Puritanism and Revolution* (London: Secker and Warburg, 1958), 32; see also Julian Cornwall, *Revolt of the Peasantry 1549* (London: Routledge and Kegan Paul, 1977), 3.

3. Geoffrey R. Elton, *Policy and Police: The Enforcement of the Reformation in the Age of Thomas Cromwell* (Cambridge: Cambridge University Press, 1972), 44.

4. J. D. Scarisbrick, *The Reformation and the English People* (Oxford: Blackwell, 1984), 170.

5. Joel Hurstfield, "The Elizabethan People in the Age of Shakespeare," *Shakespeare's World*, ed. James Sutherland and Joel Hurstfield (New York: St. Martin's Press, 1964), 39.

6. Richard L. Greaves, *Society and Religion in Elizabethan England* (Minneapolis: University of Minnesota Press, 1981), 10.

7. See W. Gordon Zeevold, *Foundations of Tudor Policy* (Cambridge: Harvard University Press, 1948), 192; Stone, *Family, Sex and Marriage*, 7; Stone, *The Crisis of the Aristocracy 1558–1641* (Oxford: Oxford University Press, Clarendon Press, 1965), 164; Geoffrey R. Elton, *Reform and Revolution: England, 1509–1558* (Cambridge: Harvard University Press, 1977), 2.

8. Peter Clark, *English Provincial Society from the Reformation to the Revolution* (Hassocks, England: Harvester Press, 1977), 144.

9. Arthur B. Ferguson, *The Articulate Citizen and the English Renaissance* (Durham, N.C.: Duke University Press, 1965), 133.

10. Lawrence Stone, "The Educational Revolution in England, 1560–1640," *Past and Present* 28 (1964): 80.

11. John Ball, *A short treatise contayning all the prinicipall grounds of christian religion*, 9th impression (1633), 165, cited in David Cressy, *Literacy and the Social Order: Reading and Writing in Tudor England* (Cambridge: Cambridge University Press, 1980), 5.

12. Joan Simon, *Education and Society in Tudor England* (Cambridge: Cambridge University Press, 1966), 168. See also Lawrence Stone, *The Causes of the English Revolution 1529–1642* (New York: Harper and Row, 1972), 110; Geoffrey R. Elton, *England Under the Tudors*, 2d ed. (London: Methuen, 1974), 224–32; Peter J. Bowden, *The Wool Trade in Tudor and Stuart England* (London: Macmillan, 1962).

13. J. E. Christopher Hill, *Reformation to Industrial Revolution: A Social and Economic History of Britain 1530–1780* (New York: Random House, 1967), 32.

14. Palliser, *Age of Elizabeth*, 27.

15. Walter Cohen, *Drama of a Nation: Public Theater in Renaissance England and Spain* (Ithaca: Cornell University Press, 1985), 180.

16. Emrys Jones, *The Origins of Shakespeare* (Oxford: Oxford University Press, Clarendon Press, 1977), 14.

17. Eagleton, *William Shakespeare*, 103.

18. David Scott Kastan, "Proud Majesty Made a Subject: Shakespeare and the Spectacle of Rule," *Shakespeare Quarterly* 37 (1986): 144.

19. Robert Weimann, "Bifold Authority in Shakespeare's Theatre," *Shakespeare Quarterly* 39 (1988): 403.

20. Mullaney, *Place of the Stage*, 21, 49.

21. Simon Shepherd, *Marlowe and the Politics of Elizabethan Theatre* (New York: St. Martin's Press, 1986), xiv; Bevington, *Tudor Drama and Politics*, 11.

22. Gosson, *Plays Confuted in Five Actions*, 184.

23. Jacques Derrida, *Dissemination*, trans. Barbara Johnson (Chicago: University of Chicago Press, 1981), 7.

24. Marjorie Garber, "'What's Past Is Prologue': Temporality and Prophecy in Shakespeare's History Plays," in *Renaissance Genres: Essays on Theory, History, and Interpretation*, ed. Barbara K. Lewalski (Cambridge: Harvard University Press, 1986), 306. See also David Scott Kastan, "The Shape of Time: Form and Value in the Shakespearean History Play," *Comparative Drama* 7 (1973–74): 272.

25. References are to *The Riverside Shakespeare*, ed. G. Blakemore Evans (Boston: Houghton Mifflin, 1974), 596–627, 630–65, 671–704. All additional references to act, scene, line are cited parenthetically in the text.

26. Holinshed, 3:156. All additional page references are cited parenthetically in the text.

27. Ornstein, *Kingdom for a Stage*, 35. The scene reveals "play hardening into reality" (John W. Blanpied, "Art and Baleful Sorcery': The Counterconsciousness of *Henry VI, Part I*," *Studies in English Literature* 15 (1975): 218.

28. Michael Manheim, *The Weak King Dilemma in the Shakespearean History Play* (Syracuse, N.Y.: Syracuse University Press, 1973), 84. See also A. L. French, "*Henry VI* and the Ghost of Richard II," *English Studies* 50, Anglo-American Supplement (1969): xxxvii–xliii.

29. David Bevington brands her "claim of pregnancy to avoid execution . . . an outrageous parody of the Virgin birth" ("The Domineering Female in *1 Henry VI*," *Shakespeare Studies* 2 [1966]: 52), and David Riggs describes her as a "virtual parody of the Marlovian prototype" (*Shakespeare's Heroical Histories*, 22, 84). Phyliss Rackin notes that Shakespeare "contrives his action to subvert the subversive female voices and ratify the masculine version of the past" ("Anti-Historians: Women's Roles in Shakespeare's Histories," *Theater Journal* 37 [1985]: 330).

30. See especially Prior, *Drama of Power;* Arthur Sewall, *Character and Society in Shakespeare* (Oxford: Oxford University Press, 1951).

31. To Don M. Ricks, Suffolk's captors represent the "most lawless element in society, . . . [a] pirate band made up of military deserters" (*Shakespeare's Emergent Form: A Study of the Structures of the "Henry VI" Plays* [Logan: Utah State University Press, 1968], 73). To the contrary, Peter Bilton argues that Walter Whitmore serves to vent the audience's disapproval of the villain Suffolk (*Commentary and Control in Shakespeare's Plays* [New York: Humanities Press,1974], 28, and Joseph Candido describes Suffolk's "posturing" as "sadly self-deflating" ("Getting Loose in the *Henry VI* Plays," *Shakespeare Quarterly* 35 [1984]: 400).

32. Ronald Berman, "Fathers and Sons in the *Henry VI* Plays," *Shakespeare Quarterly* 13 (1962): 493. To Brents Stirling the scenes represent Shakespeare's reaction to the rioting Brownists and Anabaptists of his own day (*The Populace in Shakespeare* [New York: Columbia University Press, 1949], 101); see also Richard Wilson, "'A Mingled Yarn': Shakespeare and the Cloth Workers," *Literature and History* 12 (1986): 164–80.

33. Margaret Webster, *Shakespeare Without Tears* (New York: McGraw-Hill, 1942), 122; Barry Jackson, "On Producing Shakespeare," *Shakespeare Survey* 6 (1953): 50; Wayne L. Billings, "Ironic Lapses: Plotting in *Henry VI*," *Studies in the Literary Imagination* 5 (1972): 27.

34. The emphasis is upon the infinite varieties of insatiable ambition (John Arthos, *Shakespeare: The Early Writings* [Totowa, N.J.: Rowman and Littlefield,

1972], 205) that vitiate the very concepts of justice and law (Edward I. Berry, *Patterns of Decay: Shakespeare's Early Histories* [Charlottesville: University of Virginia Press, 1975], 29.

35. On Shakespeare's misleading the audience to make York's success more startling, see Roger Warren, "'Contrarieties Agree': An Aspect of Dramatic Technique in *Henry VI*," *Shakespeare Survey* 37 (1984): 75.

36. A figure who symbolizes the "ultimate in a cultivated man" (Samuel M. Pratt, "Shakespeare and Humphrey Duke of Gloucester: A Study of Myth," *Shakespeare Quarterly*, 16 [1965]: 216), he is what Riggs calls the "type of Renaissance governor whom humanists like Ascham and Elyot saw as supplanting such medieval *chevaliers* as Talbot" (119).

37. As E. W. Talbert observes, "the attributes of vigor and Christianity are divided between York and Henry, instead of being combined, as was necessary for effective rule" (*Problem of Order*, 197).

38. From the "balanced pattern of confrontation" in the opening scenes (Robert Y. Turner, *Shakespeare's Apprenticeship* [Chicago: University of Chicago Press, 1974], 44), Shakespeare sets forth a "play of battles, each more savage than the last" (Herschel Baker, introduction to *Henry VI, Parts 1, 2, and 3*, in *The Riverside Shakespeare*, 592), in which the opposing value judgments of the rival claimants "are subsumed" and "both are valid" (Arthur Percival Rossiter, *Angel With Horns and Other Essays*, ed, Graham Storey [New York: Theatre Arts Books, 1961], 51).

39. Wolfgang Clemen notes that omens and prophecies both increase the excitement of the moment and architectonically heighten the dramatic tension by establishing a pattern of anticipation ("Anticipation and Foreboding in Shakespeare's Early Histories," *Shakespeare Survey* 6 [1953]: 26).

40. While Hugh M. Richmond's charge that Henry is a "bore" may be extreme (*Shakespeare's Political Plays* [New York: Random House, 1967], 57), one must agree that Henry has been "too simple for a politician" and "too ready to trust to conciliation to be a soldier" (Una Ellis-Fermor, *The Frontiers of Drama* [London: Methuen, 1945], 38).

41. See Faye L. Kelly, "Oaths in Shakespeare's *Henry VI* Plays," *Shakespeare Quarterly* 24 (1973): 359, and Raymond V. Utterback, "Public Men, Private Wills, and Kingship in *Henry VI, Part III*," *Renaissance Papers* (1978): 54.

42. The vision of Henry "fixed in a pose of sorrow" (Muriel C. Bradbrook, *Shakespeare and Elizabethan Poetry* [New York: Oxford University Press, 1952], 127) is "worth a thousand words" from choric figures (Bilton, 30). The ritual setting "focuses attention on the moral perversity rather than the physical horror of the crimes" (Ornstein, *Kingdom for a Stage*, 55).

43. Jan Kott, *Shakespeare Our Contemporary*, trans. Boleslaw Taborski (Garden City, N.Y.: Doubleday, 1964), 19.

Chapter 7. *King John*

1. J. L. Simmons, "Shakespeare's *King John* and Its Source: Coherence, Pattern, and Vision," *Tulane Studies in English* 17 (1969): 61.

2. Citations from *King John* are from *The Riverside Shakespeare*. All additional references are cited parenthetically by act, scene, line in the text.

3. Henry Howard Furness, Jr., *The Life and Death of King John*, A new Variorum Edition of Shakespeare (Philadelphia: Lipincott, 1919), 319.

4. As Wolfgang Clemen notes, Shakespeare masses the reports of Constance's death, Elinor's death, the barons' rebellion, and the French invasion to achieve an overwhelming effect (*Shakespeare's Dramatic Art* [London: Methuen, 1972], 105).

5. Paul Siegel has recently argued that the struggle inherent in the evolution of the classes is a central conflict in all of Shakespeare's histories ("Monarchy, Aristocracy and Bourgeoisie in Shakespeare's History Plays," *Science and Society* 42 [1978–79]: 478).

6. Cited in Furness, ed., *King John*, 319.

7. William Matchett, ed., *King John*, The Signet Classic Shakespeare (New York: New American Library, 1966), xxxi–xxxii.

8. Two distinct concepts of King John coalesced in the mind of the Elizabethan spectator: the medieval image of the tyrant and the Reformation image of the protestant martyr (John R. Elliott, Jr., "Shakespeare and the Double Image of King John," *Shakespeare Studies* 1 [1965]: 65–66; Jonathan R. Price, "*King John* and Problematic Art," *Shakespeare Quarterly* 21 [1970]: 26). "Right and wrong . . . are question-begging words" (Reese, *Cease of Majesty*, 284); the persistent "ambivalence of response . . . constitutes the central political and theatrical interest" (Richmond, *Shakespeare's Political Plays*, 100).

9. Sigurd Burckhardt, "*King John:* The Ordering of This Present Time," *ELH* 33 (1966): 149. The play, according to John Masefield, is "an intellectual form in which a number of people with obsessions illustrate the idea of treachery" (*William Shakespeare* [New York: Holt, 1911], 76); a "struggle of kingly greed and priestly pride" (Edward Dowden, *Shakespere* [London: Macmillan, 1877], 168), it reflects a "mixture of philosophic materialism and machiavellian politics" (Ronald Berman, "Anarchy and Order in *Richard III* and *King John*," *Shakespeare Survey* 20 (1967): 54). Right can only be asserted, not legitimized (David S. Kastan, "'To Set a Form Upon That Indigest': Shakespeare's Fictions of History," *Comparative Drama* 17 [1983]: 9).

10. John W. Blanpied, *Time and the Artist in Shakespeare's English Histories* (Newark: University of Delaware Press, 1983), 118.

11. Virginia Mason Vaughan, "Between Tetralogies: *King John* as Transition," *Shakespeare Quarterly* 35 (1984): 419.

12. See my *Perspective in Shakespeare's English Histories* (Athens: University of Georgia Press, 1980), 97–98.

13. Manheim, *Weak King Dilemma*, 131. If to call John a tragic figure is an exaggeration (Charles Stubblefield, "Some Thoughts About *King John*," *College English Association Critic* 35, no. 3 (1973): 27), it is also misleading to claim that as a usurper he forfeits all sympathy" (John Dover Wilson, ed. *King John* [Cambridge: Cambridge University Press, 1954], xliv).

14. Ribner, *English History Play*, 122; Adrien Bonjour, "The Road to Swinstead Abbey," *ELH* 18 (1951): 265.

15. Sidney C. Burgoyne, "Cardinal Pandulph and the Curse of Rome," *College Literature* 4 (1977): 238. Topical critics are especially attracted to this scene as a parallel to Jesuitical equivocation (Reese, *Cease of Majesty*, 272; E. A. J. Honigmann, ed., *King John*, The Arden Shakespeare [London: Methuen, 1954], 69n.) or the advice to Philip of Spain to await Mary's death before expecting papal support for his cause (Campbell, *Shakespeare's "Histories,"* 147).

16. Matchett, ed., *King John*, xxxvi.

17. James L. Calderwood, "Commodity and Honour in *King John*," *University of Toronto Quarterly* 29 (1960): 355. Emrys Jones finds a structural parallel in

Mundus et Infans, in which the moral innocent must encounter the world of experience (*Origins of Shakespeare,* 235). Julia C. Van de Water sees him as two separate characters, a Vice in the first three acts and a patriot in the last two ("The Bastard in *King John,*" *Shakespeare Quarterly* 11 [1960]: 143), and to Frank P. Wilson he is a split Shakespearean personality leading to both Falstaff and Hal (*Shakespearian and Other Studies,* ed. Helen Gardner [Oxford: Oxford University Press, Clarendon Press, 1969], 38). Jacqueline Trace, who suggests a sixteenth-century source for the figure, speaks of his "becoming an able statesman and a man of compassion and faith through the course of the play" ("Shakespeare's Bastard Faulconbridge: An Early Tudor Hero," *Shakespeare Studies* 13 [1980]: 65).

18. Blanpied, *Time,* 105. Branded a "crude materialist" by Gunnar Boklund ("The Troublesome Ending of *King John,*" *Studia Neophilologica* 40 [1968]: 177), he, according to Ronald Stroud, "must either embrace the erring obsessions of his world or remain a moral 'bastard'" ("The Bastard to the Time in *King John,*" *Comparative Drama* 6 [1972]: 155). He sets his character for us when he "frankly admits to cynical role-playing" in his commodity speech (Douglas Wixon, "'Calm Words Folded Up in Smoke': Propaganda and Spectator Response in *King John,*" *Shakespeare Studies* 14 [1981]: 111).

19. Eugene Waith, "*King John* and the Drama of History," *Shakespeare Quarterly* 29 (1978): 211.

20. Kastan, "To Set a Form," 14.

21. Citations from *1, 2 The Troublesome Reign of King John* are from the edition of Geoffrey Bullough, *Narrative and Dramatic Sources of Shakespeare,* vol. 4 (London: Routledge and Kegan Paul, 1962), 72–151. All additional references are cited by line number parenthetically in the text.

22. Citations from Raphael Holinshed's *Chronicles of England, Scotland, and Ireland* are from Bullough, *Narrative,* 4:25–49. All additional references are cited by page parenthetically in the text.

23. That each of these narrative elements is present in both Holinshed and *The Troublesome Reign* but absent in Shakespeare strongly supports the assumption that *The Troublesome Reign* is a source of Shakespeare's play, not the reverse. Similar events include the intention of the defecting English nobles to crown Lewis as king of England (in Shakespeare the lords merely join the invading force) and Pandulph's arrival with news of John's subjection to the church before Lewis and his forces have sailed from France (in Shakespeare the invasion is well underway).

24. Leonard Dean, "Tudor Theories of History Writing," *University of Michigan Contributions in Modern Philology* 1 (1947): 4.

25. Bullough, *Narrative,* 4:8.

26. J. Philip Brockbank, "The Frame of Disorder—*Henry VI,*" in *Early Shakespeare,* ed. John Russell Brown and Bernard Harris (London: Arnold, 1961), 75.

27. Eamon Grennan, "Shakespeare's Satirical History," *Shakespeare Studies* 11 (1978): 34. Grennan's argument is that Shakespeare, by so obviously and blatantly transforming the Bastard from the role of satirist and parodist to that of the official mouthpiece of patriotism, forces us to question the very essence of teleological history. On the active role of the spectator in *King John,* see also Wixon, "Calm Words," 112–21, and Blanpied, *Time,* 119.

28. Grennan, "Satirical History," 21. The play is "a bridge, a transition" (Sidney Shanker, *Shakespeare and the Uses of Ideology* [The Hague: Mouton, 1975], 56), an "experimental play between two tetralogies" (Robert B. Pierce, *Shakespeare's*

History Plays: The Family and the State [Columbus: Ohio State University Press, 1971], 125). S. C. Sen Gupta describes it as "a new kind of historical drama, in which the dramatist projects an idea through the interaction of plot and character" (Shakespeare's Historical Plays [London: Oxford University Press, 1964], 98). See also Champion, Perspective, 110.

    29. James L. Calderwood, "Creative Uncreation in King Lear," Shakespeare Quarterly 37 (1986): 17.

Chapter 8. Richard II

    1. Holinshed, Chronicles 2:746. All additional references are cited parenthetically by volume and page number in the text.

    2. Cited in Peter Ure, ed., King Richard II (London: Methuen, 1965), lix.

    3. Tillyard, Shakespeare's History Plays, 12.

    4. Derek Traversi, Shakespeare: From "Richard II" to "Henry V" (Stanford, Calif.: Stanford California Press, 1957), 12. The view persists in the recent assertion by Robert R. Reed that "Shakespeare intended to show his audience (in contrast to our skeptical selves) . . . the control of providence, even though the acts are ostensibly those of men, over the world of the play" (Crime and God's Judgment in Shakespeare [Lexington: University Press of Kentucky, 1984], 6). Alfred Hart claims that a medieval concept of the divine right of kings is "historically false" and that Shakespeare and his colleagues "drew their allusions to the doctrines" from the Tudor-inspired Book of Homilies (Shakespeare and the Homilies, 68, 73). John N. Figgis points out, however, that Wycliffe's writings in defense of imperialism and the general struggle against the papacy did lead Richard to "claim for himself the position of an absolute monarch by Divine Right" (The Divine Right of Kings [Cambridge: Cambridge University Press, 1896], 73). By contrast, the driving force in the development of divine right during the Tudor era was not the need for antipapal theory but the desire for an omnipotent crown in parliament (John W. Allen, A History of Political Thought in the Sixteenth Century [London: Methuen, 1928], 169).

    5. Ribner, English History Play, 154.

    6. Holderness, Potter, and Turner, Play, 32.

    7. Graham Holderness "Shakespeare's History: Richard II," Literature and History 7 (1981): 19.

    8. Holderness, Potter, and Turner, Play, 24.

    9. See, for example, Rossiter, Angel With Horns, 292.

    10. On the one hand, Bullingbrook is seen as "a manifestation of . . . the acutal Machiavellian philosophy" (Irving Ribner, "Bolingbroke, A True Machiavellian," Modern Language Quarterly, 9 [1948]: 178), a "schemer" whose "speeches . . . betray calculation in their over-humility, over-sweetness" (R. F. Hill, "Dramatic Techniques and Interpretation in Richard II," in Early Shakespeare, ed. John Russell Brown and Bernard Harris [New York: St. Martin's Press, 1961], 115). On the other hand, he is "an instrument in the hands of Providence" (Georges A. Bonnard, "The Actor in Richard II," Shakespeare Jahrbuch 82 [1951]: 89), an opportunist (Brents Stirling, "Bolingbroke's Decision," Shakespeare Quarterly 2 [1951]: 30) who thought of deposition only when Richard suggested it to him (A. L. French, "Who Deposed Richard II?" Essays in Criticism 17 [1967], 424). There is guilt in Hereford, to be sure, yet he "is certainly meant to be admired"

(Patrick Crutwell, *The Shakespearean Moment* [New York: Random House, 1960], 197).

11. As Ronald B. MacDonald has recently noted, the excessive vocabulary of divine right does not in fact suggest that the king "really *is* supreme and untouchable, but [that he is] patently vulnerable" ("Uneasy Lies: Language and History in Shakespeare's Lancastrian Tetralogy," *Shakespeare Quarterly* 35 [1984]: 23). The "sign" becomes a "fetish, shorn of a significant context" (Eagleton, *William Shakespeare*, 8, 15). "In assuming the authority of blood is absolute, Richard neglects those displays of political authority which establish the absolute power of the monarch over the material body of the subject" (Tennenhouse, *Power on Display* 77).

12. References are to *The Riverside Shakespeare*, 805–37. All additonal references are cited parenthetically by act, scene, line in the text.

13. Barbara D. Palmer, "'Ciphers to This Great Accompt': Civic Pageantry in the Second Tetralogy," in *Pageantry in the Shakespearean Theater*, ed. David M. Bergeron (Athens: University of Georgia Press, 1985), 118.

14. Maurice Keen, *Chivalry* (New Haven: Yale University Press, 1984), 247.

15. Henry C. Lea, *Superstition and Force* (1870; New York: Greenwood Press, 1968), 171.

16. Ibid., 195.

17. William S. Holdsworth, *History of English Law*, 3d ed. (London: Methuen, 1922), 3:290.

18. J. G. Bellamy, *The Law of Treason in England in the Later Middle Ages* (Cambridge: Cambridge University Press, 1970), 87.

19. Maude Violet Clark, *Fourteenth Century Studies*, ed. L.S. Sutherland and M. McKissack (Oxford: Oxford University Press, 1937), 132.

20. *Historical Manuscripts Commission*, 8th Report, appendix, pt. 1, sec. 2, no. 267; cited in Bellamy, *Law of Treason*, 102.

21. Bellamy, *Law of Treason*, 107; emphasis mine.

22. George Drewry Squibb, *The High Court of Chivalry* (Oxford: Oxford University Press, Clarendon Press, 1959), 23.

23. Peter Saccio, *Shakespeare's English Kings* (Oxford: Oxford University Press, 1977), 26.

24. Harry Berger, "Psychoanalyzing the Shakespeare Text: The First Three Scenes of the *Henriad*," in *Shakespeare and the Question of Theory*, ed. Patricia Parker and Geoffrey Hartman (New Haven: Yale University Press, 1985), 215.

25. Paul Gaudet notes that, whereas in Holinshed the parasites openly display their villainy and hence their guilt, Shakespeare's technique is more allusive, their guilt more problematic. Consequently, there is an undeniable touch of the equivocal and self-righteous in Bullingbrook's peremptory pronouncements and actions ("The 'Parasitical' Counsellors in Shakespeare's *Richard II:* A Problem in Dramatic Interpretation," *Shakespeare Quarterly* 33 [1982]: 144).

26. By this point the challenge to combat has become a "political tool through which courtiers may provide a show of allegiance to Bolingbroke" (Henry E. Jacobs, "Prophecy and Ideology in Shakespeare's *Richard II*," *South Atlantic Review* 51 [1986]: 3).

27. According to Holinshed, Northumberland persuaded Richard, with the understanding that Bullingbrook would lay down his arms, to leave Conway Castle in order to assemble a parliament in which Bullingbrook would be pardoned and "in which iustice might be had, against such as were enimies to the commonwealth" (*Chronicles*, 2:856). Northumberland, however, had prepared an ambush, and Richard was delivered into Bullingbrook's power at Flint Castle.

"The Noise of Threatening Drum"

Here Shakespeare markedly departs from the historical record in order
~hasize Bullingbrook's action as that of an absolute monarch. In Holinshed
~rliament of 1399 pronounced many charges against Richard, and "in open
pa~. ment, it was thought by the most part, that he was worthie to be deposed
from all kinglie honor and princelie gouernment" (*Chronicles*, 2:861). The terms
of Richard's deposition were approved by both the lords and the commoners,
and it was only after parliamentary approval that Hereford was crowned king.

29. Greenblatt, *Shakespearean Negotiations* (Berkeley: University of California
Press, 1988), 8.

30. Phyliss Rackin, "The Role of the Audience in Shakespeare's *Richard II*,"
Shakespeare Quarterly 36 (1985): 281.

Chapter 9. The *Henriad*

1. Gary Taylor, *To Analyze Delight* (Newark: University of Delaware Press,
1985), 158.

2. Gareth Lloyd Evans, "Shakespeare, the Twentieth Century and Behaviourism," *Shakespeare Survey* 20 (1967): 139.

3. Derek Cohen, *Shakespearean Motives* (New York: St. Martin's Press, 1987),
24.

4. Tillyard, *Shakespeare's History Plays;* Reed, *Crime and God's Judgment* 6.

5. Greenblatt, "Invisible Bullets," 20. As Dollimore observes, the Renaissance was an age engaged in intensive interrogation of its received ideas (*Radical
Shakespeare* [Chicago: University of Chicago Press, 1984], 10).

6. David Bevington, ed., *Henry IV, Part 1*, The Oxford Shakespeare (Oxford:
Oxford University Press, 1987), 49.

7. All citations to Shakespeare's plays refer to *The Riverside Shakespeare*. Additional references are cited parenthetically by act, scene, line in the text.

8. Holderness, Potter, and Turner, *Play*, 59. "In the world after the usurpation, the head that wears the crown will always lie, however uneasily, for possession of the crown depends upon a fabrication" MacDonald, "Uneasy Lies," 39);
the demonstration of these acts "is rendered an entertainment for which an audience, subject to just this State, will pay money and applaud" (Greenblatt, "Invisible Bullets," 39).

9. Machiavelli, *Discourses*, 147.

10. Jonathan Dollimore and Alan Sinfield, "History and Ideology: The Instance of *Henry V*," in *Alternative Shakespeares*, ed. John Drakakis (London: Methuen, 1985), 211–12.

11. Stephen Greenblatt, *Shakespearean Negotiations: The Circulation of Social Energy in the Renaissance* (Berkeley: University of California Press, 1988), 137.

12. Niccolo Machiavelli, *The Prince*, trans. Robert Caponigri (Chicago: Henry
Regnery, 1963), 118.

13. A. R. Humphreys, ed., *2 Henry IV*, the Arden Shakespeare (London: Methuen, 1960), 242.

14. Citations, by volume and page number, refer to Holinshed, *Chronicles*.

15. As Lawrence Danson says of Hal's later career, "Perhaps it is not just the
king's choice but the actorly manner of his choosing that makes us uncomfortable" ("*Henry V:* King, Chorus, and Critics," *Shakespeare Quarterly* 34 [1983]: 37).
Hal intends progressively "to reinvest the royal name with meaning" (Joseph
Candido, "The Name of King: Hal's Titles in the *Henriad*," *Texas Studies in Literature and Language* 26 [1984]: 63). See also Norman Sanders, "The True Prince

and the False Thief: Prince Hal and the Shift of Identity," *Shakespeare Survey* 30 [1977]: 29–34). Through such decension from prince to prentice, Steven Mullaney argues, Hal reflects "a culture in the process of extending its boundaries and reformulating itself" ("Strange Things, Gross Terms, Curious Customs: The Rehearsal of Cultures in the Late Renaissance," in *Representing the English Renaissance*, ed. Stephen Greenblatt [Berkeley: University of California Press, 1988], 84).

16. For a sampling of critical views see my *Perspective in Shakespeare's English Histories*, 207, n. 40. Social critics find Falstaff's origins in figures from the London streets of Shakespeare's day (Paul N. Siegel, "Falstaff and His Social Milieu," *Shakespeare Jahrbuch* 110 [1974]: 139), in the impoverished gentry sinking into decadence with the disintegration of feudalism (T. A. Jackson, "Marx and Shakespeare," *Labour Monthly* 46 [1964]: 165–73), or, conversely, in the opportunist who emerged in society following such a transition (Axel Clark, "The Battle of Shrewsbury," *Critical Quarterly* 15 [1972]: 29–45). In any case he functions in the play to subvert social order as a self-serving hedonist who "refuses to be inscribed by social imperatives" (Eagleton, *Shakespeare*, 16).

17. Tennenhouse, *Power on Display*, 83.

18. Ibid., 79, 83.

19. Bristol, *Carnival and Theater: Plebeian Culture and the Structure of Authority in Renaissance England* (London: Methuen, 1985), 22.

20. Greenblatt, "Invisible Bullets," 31. Claims that Francis is a parody of Hotspur (J. McLaverty, "No Abuse: The Prince and Falstaff in the Tavern Scenes of *Henry IV*," *Shakespeare Survey* 34 [1981]: 107), that Hal puts the drawer analogously into his own position of being drawn simultaneously by the court and the tavern (J. D. Schucter, "Prince Hal and Francis: The Imitation of an Action," *Shakespeare Studies* 3 [1967]: 129–37), or that the scene serves as a comic catharsis for Hal, purging him of "this 'base' association" (Gerard H. Cox, "'Like a Prince Indeed': Hal's Triumph of Honor in *1 Henry IV*," in *Pageantry in the Shakespearean Theater*, ed. David M. Bergeron [Athens: University of Georgia Press, 1985], 138) are more ingenious than convincing.

21. Irving Ribner, "The Political Problems in Shakespeare's Lancastrian Tetralogy," *Studies in Philology* 49 (1952): 183; G. Wilson Knight brands it "a dastardly example of treachery" (*The Olive and the Sword* [London: Oxford University Press, 1944], 27).

22. Tillyard, *History Plays*, 345.

23. John Dover Wilson, ed. *King Henry IV* (Cambridge: Cambridge University Press, 1955), xiv.

24. J. H. Walter, ed., *King Henry V*, The Arden Shakespeare (London: Methuen, 1954), xxiii.

25. Theodore Weiss, *The Breath of Clowns and Kings* (New York: Atheneum, 1971), 296.

26. John F. Danby, *Shakespeare's Doctrine of Nature* (London: Faber and Faber, 1949), 90.

27. William Hazlitt, *Characters of Shakespeare's Plays*, 3d ed. (London: Templeman, 1838), 206.

28. William Butler Yeats, *Ideas of Good and Evil* (London: Bullen, 1903), 163.

29. C. H. Hobday, "Image and Irony in *Henry V*," *Shakespeare Survey* 21 (1968): 109.

30. John Masefield, *William Shakespeare* (New York: Holt, 1911), 122.

31. John Bromley, *The Shakespearean Kings* (Boulder: Colorado Associated University Press, 1971), 85.

32. Andrew Cecil Bradley, *Oxford Lectures on Poetry*, 2d ed. (London: Macmillan, 1909), 257.

33. Ellis-Fermor, *Frontiers of Drama*, 47.

34. Manheim, *Weak King Dilemma*, 167.

35. "The Purpose of Playing: Reflections on a Shakespearean Anthropology," *Helius* n.s. 7 (1980): 57.

36. Norman Rabkin argues that the play forces us to "hold in balance incompatible and radically opposed views each of which seems exclusively true" ("Rabbits, Ducks, and *Henry V*," *Shakespeare Quarterly* 28 [1977]: 294).

37. Dollimore and Sinfield, "History and Ideology," 221.

38. Greenblatt, *Negotiations*, 138.

39. Anthony S. Brennan, "That Within Which Passes Show: The Function of the Chorus in *Henry V*," *Philological Quarterly* 58 (1979): 47.

40. "Williams' common-sense defense of his actions, his readiness to suggest that the king is at fault, discomfort Henry by reducing him to the level of 'a common man' at a time, and in a place, where it does not suit his convenience" (Paul Dean, "Chronicle and Romance Modes in *Henry V*," *Shakespeare Quarterly* 36 [1985]: 73).

41. See Karl P. Wentersdorf, "The Conspiracy of Silence in *Henry V*," *Shakespeare Quarterly* 27 (1976): 280, 283.

42. Adrian Noble's Royal Shakespeare Company production in 1984 highlighted this irony by having Bardolph, hands tied behind his back, garroted on stage, where he remained through the entire scene, with blood dripping occasionally from his mouth (Alan C. Dessen, "Staging Shakespeare's History Plays in 1984: A Tale of Three Henrys," *Shakespeare Quarterly* 36 [1985]: 73).

43. Holderness, *Shakespeare's History*, 77.

44. Richard Levin, *The Multiple Plot in English Renaissance Drama* (Chicago: University of Chicago Press, 1971), 16, 116.

45. Gunter Walch, "*Henry V* as Working-House of Ideology," *Shakespeare Survey* 40 (1988): 68; the juxtaposition of a Henry living in the world of history with the king "shining in the world of the Chorus' creation" forces the play to ask "new and shocking" ideological questions (67).

Conclusion

1. Raymond Williams, afterword, *Political Shakespeare*, ed. Jonathan Dollimore and Alan Sinfield (Ithaca: Cornell University Press, 1985), 238.

2. Patterson, *Censorship and Interpretation*, 17.

3. James H. Kavanagh, "Shakespeare in Ideology," in *Alternative Shakespeares*, ed. John Drakakis (London: Methuen, 1985), 151.

4. Thomas Dekker, *The Gvls Horne-booke*, in *The Non-Dramatic Works of Thomas Dekker*, ed Alexander Grossart (London: privately printed, 1884), 2:247.

5. Jonathan Dollimore and Alan Sinfield, "History and Ideology: The Instance of *Henry V*," in *Alternative Shakespeares*, 211.

6. F. Smith Fussner, *The Historical Revolution: English Historical Writing and Thought 1580–1640* (London: Routledge and Kegan Paul, 1962), 300.

7. Arthur B. Ferguson, *The Articulate Citizen and the English Renaissance* (Durham, N.C.: Duke University Press, 1965), 401.

8. F. Smith Fussner, *Tudor History and the Historians* (New York: Basic Books, 1970), 237.

9. Fussner, *Revolution*, 311.

10. Stephen Toulmin and June Goodfield, *The Discovery of Time* (New York: Harper and Row, 1965), 15.

11. Holderness, Potter, and Turner, *Shakespeare: The Play of History*, 19.

12. Derek Longhurst, "'Not For All Time, But For an Age': An Approach to Shakespeare Studies," in *Re-Reading English*, ed. Peter Widdowson (London: Methuen, 1982), 159.

13. Williams, 230.

Bibliography

Acheson, Arthur. *Shakespeare, Chapman, and Sir Thomas More*. New York: Hackett, 1931.

Adams, Joseph Quincy, ed. *The Famous Victories of Henry V*. Boston: Houghton Mifflin, 1924.

Allen, John W. *A History of Political Thought in the Sixteenth Century*. London: Methuen, 1928.

Armstrong, Ray Livingstone, ed. *The Raigne of King Edward III*. In *Six Plays Related to the Shakespeare Canon*, edited by Ephraim B. Everitt and R. L. Armstrong. Copenhagen: Rosenkilde and Bagger, 1965.

Armstrong, William Alvin. *Elizabethan History Plays*. London: Oxford University Press, 1965.

Arthos, John. *Shakespeare: The Early Writings*. Totowa, N.J.: Rowman and Littlefield, 1972.

Baker, Herschel. Introduction to *Henry VI, Parts 1, 2, and 3*, in *The Riverside Shakespeare*, edited by G. Blakemore Evans. Boston: Houghton Mifflin, 1974.

Bell, Mary. "*Edward III*." M.A. thesis. University of Liverpool, 1959.

Bellamy, J. G. *The Law of Treason in England in the Later Middle Ages*. Cambridge: Cambridge University Press, 1970.

Bentley, Gerald Eades. *The Jacobean and Caroline Stage*. 6 vols. Oxford: Oxford University Press, Clarendon Press, 1941–68.

Berger, Harry, "Psychoanalyzing the Shakespeare Text: The First Three Scenes of the *Henriad*." In *Shakespeare and the Question of Theory*, edited by Patricia Parker and Geoffrey Hartman. New Haven: Yale University Press, 1985.

Berman, Ronald. "Anarchy and Order in *Richard III* and *King John*." *Shakespeare Survey* 20 (1967): 51–60.

———. "Fathers and sons in the *Henry VI* Plays." *Shakespeare Quarterly* 13 (1962): 487–97.

Berry, Edward I. *Patterns of Decay: Shakespeare's Early Histories*. Charlottesville: University of Virginia Press, 1975.

Bevington, David. "The Domineering Female in *1 Henry VI*." *Shakespeare Studies* 2 (1966): 51–58.

———. *Tudor Drama and Politics*. Cambridge: Harvard University Press, 1968.

———, ed. *Henry IV, Part I*. The Oxford Shakespeare. Oxford: Oxford University Press, 1987.

Billings, Wayne L. "Ironic Lapses: Plotting in *Henry VI*." *Studies in the Literary Imagination* 5 (1972): 27–49.

Bilton, Peter. *Commentary and Control in Shakespeare's Plays*. New York: Humanities Press, 1974.

Blanpied, John W. "'Art and Baleful Sorcery': The Counterconsciousness of *Henry VI, Part I*." *Studies in English Literature* 15 (1975): 213–27.

———. *Time and the Artist in Shakespeare's English Histories*. Newark: University of Delaware Press, 1983.

Boas, Frederick S. *An Introduction to Tudor Drama*. Oxford: Oxford University Press, Clarendon Press, 1933.

———. *Shakespeare and the Universities*. New York: Appleton, 1923.

Boklund, Gunnar. "The Troublesome Ending of *King John*." *Studia Neophilologica* 40 (1968): 175–84.

Bonjour, Adrien. "The Road to Swinstead Abbey." *ELH* 18 (1951): 253–74.

Bonnard, Georges A. "The Actor in *Richard II*." *Shakespeare Jahrbuch* 82 (1951): 87–101.

Booth, Stephen. Review of *The Privileged Playgoers of Shakespeare's London, 1576–1640*, by Ann Jennalie Cook. *Medieval and Renaissance Drama in England* 2 (1985): 306–11.

Boswell, Eleanor, ed. *Edmund Ironside*. The Malone Society Reprints. Oxford: Oxford University Press, 1928.

Bowden, Peter J. *The Wool Trade in Tudor and Stuart England*. London: Macmillan, 1962.

Bradbrook, Muriel C. *The Growth and Structure of Elizabethan Comedy*. London: Chatto and Windus, 1955.

———. *Shakespeare and Elizabethan Poetry*. New York: Oxford University Press, 1952.

Bradley, Andrew Cecil. *Oxford Lectures on Poetry*. 2d ed. London: Macmillan, 1909.

Brennan, Anthony S. "That Within Which Passeth Show: The Function of the Chorus in *Henry V*." *Philological Quarterly* 58 (1979): 40–52.

Briggs, Julia. *This Stage-Play World*. Oxford: Oxford University Press, 1983.

Bristol, Michael D. *Carnival and Theater: Plebeian Culture and the Structure of Authority in Renaissance England*. London: Methuen, 1985.

Brockbank, J. Philip. "The Frame of Disorder—*Henry VI*." In *Early Shakespeare*, edited by John Russell Brown and Bernard Harris. London: Arnold, 1961.

Bromley, John. *The Shakespearean Kings*. Boulder: Colorado Associated University Press, 1971.

Brooke, C. F. Tucker, *The Shakespeare Apocrypha*. Oxford: Oxford University Press, Clarendon Press, 1918.

———. *The Tudor Drama*. Boston: Houghton Mifflin, 1911.

Bullen, Arthur Henry. *A Collection of Old English Plays*. 4 vols. London: Wyman, 1882.

Bullough, Geoffrey. "Pre-Conquest History Themes in Elizabethan Drama." In *Medieval Literature and Civilisation*, edited by D. A. Pearsall and R. A. Waldron. London: Atlhone Press, 1969.

Burckhardt, Sigurd. "*King John:* The Ordering of This Present Time." *ELH* 33 (1966): 133–53.

Burgoyne, Signey C. "Cardinal Pandulph and the Curse of Rome." *College Literature* 4 (1977): 232–40.

Butler, Martin. *Theater in Crisis, 1632–1642.* Cambridge: Cambridge University Press, 1970.

Calderwood, James L. "Commodity and Honour in *King John.*" *University of Toronto Quarterly* 29 (1960): 341–56.

———. "Creative Uncreation in *King Lear.*" *Shakespeare Quarterly* 37 (1986): 5–19.

Campbell, Lily B. *Shakespeare's "Histories."* San Marino, Calif.: Huntington Library Press, 1947.

Candido, Joseph. "Getting Loose in the *Henry VI* Plays." *Shakespeare Quarterly* 35 (1984): 392–406.

———. "The Name of King: Hal's Titles in the *Henriad.*" *Texas Studies in Literature and Language* 26 (1984): 61–73.

Chambers, Edmund K. *The Elizabethan Stage.* 4 vols. Oxford: Oxford University Press, Clarendon Press, 1923.

———. *William Shakespeare: Facts and Problems.* 2 vols. Oxford: Oxford University Press, Clarendon Press, 1930.

Champion, Larry S. *Perspective in Shakespeare's History Plays.* Athens: University of Georgia Press, 1980.

Charlton, Henry Buckley. *Shakespeare, Politics and Politicians.* English Association Pamphlet 72. Oxford: Oxford University Press, 1929.

Clark, Axel. "The Battle of Shrewsbury." *Critical Quarterly* 15 (1972): 29–45.

Clark, Maude Violet. *Fourteenth Century Studies.* Edited by L. S. Sutherland and M. McKissack. Oxford: Oxford University Press, 1937.

Clark, Peter. *English Provincial Society from the Reformation to the Revolution.* Hassocks, England: Harvester Press, 1977.

Clemen, Wolfgang. "Anticipation and Foreboding in Shakespeare's Early Histories." *Shakespeare Survey* 6 (1953): 25–35.

———. *Shakespeare's Dramatic Art.* London: Methuen, 1972.

Cohen, Derek. *Shakespearean Motives.* New York: St. Martin's Press, 1987.

Cohen, Walter. *Drama of a Nation: Public Theater in Renaissance England and Spain.* Ithaca: Cornell University Press, 1985.

Coleridge, Samuel Taylor. *The Literary Remains of Samuel Taylor Coleridge.* Edited by Henry Nelson Coleridge. 4 vols. London: Pickering, 1836–39.

Cook, Ann Jennalie. *The Privileged Playgoers of Shakespeare's London, 1576–1640.* Princeton: Princeton University Press, 1981.

Cornwall, Julian. *Revolt of the Peasantry 1549.* London: Routledge and Kegan Paul, 1977.

Cox, Gerard H. "'Like a Prince Indeed': Hal's Triumph of Honor in *1 Henry IV.*" In *Pageantry in the Shakespearean Theater,* edited by David M. Bergeron. Athens: University of Georgia Press, 1985.

Creizenach, Wilheim. *The English Drama in the Age of Shakespeare.* London: Sidgwick and Jackson, 1926.

Cressy, David. *Literacy and the Social Order: Reading and Writing in Tudor England.* Cambridge: Cambridge University Press, 1980.

Crutwell, Patrick. *The Shakespearean Moment.* New York: Random House, 1960.

Danby, John F. *Shakespeare's Doctrine of Nature.* London: Faber and Faber, 1949.

Danson, Lawrence, "*Henry V:* King, Chorus, and Critics." *Shakespeare Quarterly* 34 (1983): 27–43.

Dean, Leonard. "Tudor Theories of History Writing." *University of Michigan Contributions in Modern Philology* 1 (1947): 1–13.

Dean, Paul. "Chronicle and Romance Modes in *Henry V.*" *Shakespeare Quarterly* 36 (1985): 18–27.

Dekker, Thomas. *The Gvls Horne-booke.* In *The Non-Dramatic Works of Thomas Dekker,* edited by Alexander Grossart, vol. 2. London: Privately Printed, 1884.

Derrida, Jacques. *Dissemination.* Translated by Barbara Johnson. Chicago: University of Chicago Press, 1981.

Dessen, Alan C. "Staging Shakespeare's History Plays in 1984: A Tale of Three Henrys." *Shakespeare Quarterly* 36 (1985): 71–79.

Dodds, M. Hope. "Edmund Ironside and *The Love-Sick King.*" *Modern Language Review* 19 (24): 158–68.

Dollimore, Jonathan. *Radical Shakespeare.* Chicago: University of Chicago Press, 1985.

Dollimore, Jonathan, and Alan Sinfield. "History and Ideology: The Instance of *Henry V.*" In *Alternative Shakespeares,* edited by John Drakakis. London: Methuen, 1985.

———, eds. *Political Shakespeare.* Ithaca: Cornell University Press, 1985.

Doran, Madeleine. *Endeavors of Art: A Study of Form in Elizabethan Drama.* Madison: University of Wisconsin Press, 1954.

Dowden, Edward. *Shakespeare.* London: Macmillan, 1877.

"Dramatic Records of the City of London: The Remembrancia." *Malone Society Collections,* vol. 1, pt. 1, edited by Edmund K. Chambers and Walter Wilson Greg. Oxford: Oxford University Press, 1908.

Eagleton, Terry. *William Shakespeare.* Oxford: Blackwell, 1986.

Elliott, John R., Jr. "Shakespeare and the Double Image of King John." *Shakespeare Studies* 1 (1965): 64–84.

Ellis-Fermor, Una. *The Frontiers of Drama* London: Methuen, 1945.

Elton, Geoffrey R. *England Under the Tudors.* 2d ed. London: Methuen, 1974.

———. *Policy and Police: The Enforcement of the Revolution in the Age of Thomas Cromwell.* Cambridge: Cambridge University Press, 1972.

———. *Reform and Revolution: England, 1509–1558.* Cambridge: Harvard University Press, 1977.

Evans, Gareth Lloyd. "Shakespeare, the Twentieth Century and Behaviourism." *Shakespeare Survey* 20 (1967): 133–42.

Evans, Ifor. *A Short History of English Drama.* Harmondsworth, England: Penguin, 1940.

Evans, Malcolm. *Signifying Nothing: Truth's True Contents in Shakespeare's Texts.* Athens: University of Georgia Press, 1986.

Everitt, Ephraim B. *The Young Shakespeare: Studies in Documentary Evidence.* Copenhagen: Rosenkilde and Bagger, 1954.

Farjeon, Herbert, ed. *The Raigne of Edward III.* In *The Complete Works of Shakespeare.* New York: Nonesuch Press, 1929.

Farnham, Willard. *The Medieval Heritage of Elizabethan Tragedy.* Oxford: Blackwell, 1936.

Ferguson, Arthur B. *The Articulate Citizen and the English Renaissance.* Durham, N.C.: Duke University Press, 1965.

Figgis, John Neville. *The Divine Right of Kings.* Cambridge: Cambridge University Press, 1896.

Fleay, Frederick Gard. *A Biographical Chronicle of the English Drama 1559–1642.* London: Reeves and Turner, 1891.

Foucault, Michel. *Discipline and Punish: The Birth of the Prison.* Translated by A. Sheridan. New York: Pantheon, 1977.

Foxe, John. *The Acts and Monuments of John Foxe.* Edited by Stephen Reed Cattley. 8 vols. London: Seeley and Burnside, 1838.

French, A. L. "*Henry VI* and the Ghost of Richard II." *English Studies* 50, Anglo-American Supplement (1969): xxxvii–xliii.

———. "Who Deposed Richard II?" *Essays in Criticism* 17 (1967): 411–33.

Furness, Henry Howard, Jr., ed. Introduction to *The Life and Death of King John.* A New Variorum Edition of Shakespeare. Philadelphia: Lippincott, 1919.

Fussner, F. Smith. *The Historical Revolution: English Historical Writing and Thought 1580–1640.* London: Routledge and Kegan Paul, 1962.

———. *Tudor History and the Historians.* New York: Basic Books, 1970.

Garber, Marjorie. "'What's Past Is Prologue': Temporality and Prophecy in Shakespeare's History Plays." In *Renaissance Genres: Essays on Theory, History, and Interpretation,* edited by Barbara K. Lewalski. Cambridge: Harvard University Press, 1986.

Gaudet, Paul. "The 'Parisitical' Counsellors in Shakespeare's *Richard II:* A Problem in Dramatic Interpretation." *Shakespeare Quarterly* 33 (1982): 142–54.

Goldberg, Jonathan. *James I and the Politics of Literature.* Baltimore: Johns Hopkins University Press, 1984.

Gosson, Stephen. *Plays Confuted in Five Actions.* in *The English Drama and Stage Under the Tudor and Stuart Princes,* edited by William C. Hazlitt. London: Whittingham and Wilkins, 1869.

Greaves, Richard L. *Society and Religion in Elizabethan England.* Minneapolis: University of Minnesota Press, 1981.

Greenblatt, Stephen. "Invisible Bullets: Renaissance Authority and Its Subversion, *Henry IV* and *Henry V.*" In *Political Shakespeare,* edited by Jonathan Dollimore and Alan Sinfield. Ithaca: Cornell University Press, 1985.

———. *Shakespearean Negotiations: The Circulation of Social Energy in Renaissance England.* Berkeley: University of California Press, 1988.

Greer, C. A. "A Lost Play the Source of Shakespeare's *Henry IV* and *Henry V.*" *Notes and Queries,* n.s. 1 (1954): 53–55.

Greg, Walter Wilson. *Dramatic Documents from the Elizabethan Playhouses.* Oxford: Oxford University Press, Clarendon Press, 1931.

Grennan, Eamon. "Shakespeare's Satirical History." *Shakespeare Studies* 11 (1978): 21–37.

Gurr, Andrew. *Playgoing in Shakespeare's London.* Cambridge: Cambridge University Press, 1987.

Hall, Walter P., and Robert G. Albion. *A History of England and the British Empire.* Boston: Ginn, 1946.

Halliwell-Phillips, James O. *A Dictionary of Old English Plays.* London: J. R. Smith, 1860.

Harbage, Alfred. *Shakespeare's Audience.* New York: Columbia University Press, 1941.

————. *Shakespeare and the Rival Traditions.* New York: Macmillan, 1952.

Harbage, Alfred, and Samuel Schoenbaum. *Annals of English Drama.* 2d ed., rev. Philadelphia: University of Pennsylvania Press, 1964.

Harrison, George B. *Elizabethan Plays and Players.* Ann Arbor: University of Michigan Press, 1956.

Hart, Alfred. *Shakespeare and the Homilies.* Melbourne: Melbourne University Press, 1934.

Hazlitt, William. *Characters of Shakespeare's Plays.* 3d ed. London: Templeman, 1838.

Henslowe, Philip. *Henslowe's Diary.* Edited by Walter Wilson Greg. 2 vols. London: Bullen, 1904.

Hill, J. E. Christopher. *Puritanism and Revolution.* London: Secker and Warburg, 1958.

————. *Reformation to Industrial Revolution: A Social and Economic History of Britain, 1530–1780.* New York: Random House, 1967.

————. *Reformation to Industrial Revolution.* New York: Random House, 1967.

Hill, R. F. "Dramatic Techniques and Interpretation in *Richard II.*" In *Early Shakespeare,* edited by John Russell Brown and Bernard Harris. New York: St. Martin's Press, 1961.

Hobday, C. H. "Image and Irony in *Henry V.*" *Shakespeare Survey* 21 (1968): 107–13.

Holderness, Graham. *Shakespeare's History.* Dublin: Gill and Macmillan, 1986.

————. "Shakespeare's History: *Richard II.*" *Literature and History* 7 (1981): 2–24.

Holderness, Graham, Nick Potter, and John Turner. *Shakespeare: The Play of History.* Iowa City: University of Iowa Press, 1987.

Holdsworth, William S. *History of English Law.* 3d ed. London: Methuen, 1922.

Holinshed, Raphael. *Holinshed's Chronicles of England, Scotland and Ireland.* 6 vols. London: Johnson, 1808.

Honigmann, E. A. J., ed. Introduction to *King John.* The Arden Shakespeare. London: Methuen, 1954.

Hopkinson, Arthur Frederick, ed. *The Life and Death of Thomas, Lord Cromwell.* London: W. E. Sims, 1891.

Howard, Jean, and Marion O'Connor, eds. *Shakespeare Reproduced: The Text in History and Ideology.* London: Methuen, 1988.

Humphreys, A. R., ed. Introduction to *2 Henry IV.* The Arden Shakespeare. London: Methuen, 1960.

Hurstfield, Joel. "The Elizabethan People in the Age of Shakespeare." In *Shakespeare's World,* edited by James Sutherland and Joel Hurstfield. New York: St. Martin's Press, 1964.

Jackson, Barry. "On Producing Shakespeare." *Shakespeare Survey* 6 (1953): 49–52.

Jackson, T. A. "Marx and Shakespeare." *Labour Monthly* 46 (1964): 165–73.

Jacobs, Henry E. "Prophecy and Ideology in Shakespeare's *Richard II.*" *South Atlantic Review* 51 (1986): 3–18.

Jones, Emrys. *The Origins of Shakespeare.* Oxford: Oxford University Press, Clarendon Press, 1977.

Kastan, David Scott. "Proud Majesty Made a Subject: Shakespeare and the Spectacle of Rule." *Shakespeare Quarterly* 37 (1986): 459–75.

———. "'To Set a Form Upon That Indigest': Shakespeare's Fictions of History." *Comparative Drama* 17 (1983): 1–16.

———. "The Shape of Time: Form and Value in The Shakespearean History Play." *Comparative Drama* 7 (1973–74): 259–77.

Keen, Maurice. *Chivalry.* New Haven: Yale University Press, 1984.

Kelly, Faye L. "Oaths in Shakespeare's *Henry VI* Plays." *Shakespeare Quarterly* 24 (1973): 357–71.

Knight, G. Wilson. *The Olive and the Sword.* London: Oxford University Press, 1944.

Koskennieme, Inna. "Themes and Imagery in *Edward III.*" *Neophilologische Mitteilungen* 65 (1964): 446–80.

Kott, Jan. *Shakespeare Our Contemporary.* Translated by Boleslaw Taborski. Garden City, N.Y.: Doubleday, 1964.

Kozlenko, William, ed. *Disputed Plays of Shakespeare.* New York: Hawthorne Books, 1974.

Lambrechts, G. "Edward III, Ouevre de Thomas Kyd." *Études Anglaises* 16 (1963): 160–74.

Lea, Henry C. *Superstition and Force.* 1870; New York: Greenwood Press, 1968.

Leech, Clifford, Review of *Shakespeare as Collaborator,* by Kenneth Muir. *Notes and Queries* n.s. 8 (1961): 156–57.

———. "The Two-Part Play: Marlowe and the Early Shakespeare." *Shakespeare Jahrbuch* 94 (1958): 90–106.

Levin, Richard. *The Multiple Plot in English Renaissance Drama.* Chicago: University of Chicago Press, 1971.

Lewis, John S. "The Rash Oath in *Edward III.*" *Allegorica* 1 (1976): 269–77.

Lindabury, Richard V. *A Study of Patriotism in the Elizabethan Drama.* Princeton: Princeton University Press, 1931.

Longhurst, Derek. "'Not For All Time, But For an Age': An Approach to Shakespeare Studies." In *Re-Reading English,* edited by Peter Widdowson. London: Methuen, 1982.

MacDonald, Ronald B. "Uneasy Lies: Language and History in Shakespeare's Lancastrian Tetralogy." *Shakespeare Quarterly* 35 (1984): 22–39.

Machiavelli, Niccolo. *Discourses.* Translated by Christian Detmold. New York: Random House, 1950.

———. *The Prince.* Translated by Robert Caponigri. Chicago: Henry Regnery, 1963.

McLaverty, J. "No Abuse: The Prince and Falstaff in the Tavern Scenes of *Henry IV.*" *Shakespeare Survey* 34 (1981): 105–10.

Manheim, Michael. *The Weak King Dilemma in the Shakespearean History Play.* Syracuse, N.Y.: Syracuse University Press, 1973.

Marriott, John Arthur Ransome. *English History in Shakespeare*. London: Chapman and Hall, 1918.

Masefield, John. *William Shakespeare*. New York: Holt, 1911.

Matchett, William, ed. Introduction to *King John*. The Signet Classic Shakespeare. New York: New American Library, 1966.

Maxwell, Baldwin. *Studies in the Shakespeare Apocrypha*. New York: Columbia University Press, King's Crown Press, 1956.

Mincoff, Marco. Review of *Shakespeare as Collaborator*, by Kenneth Muir. *English Studies* 43 (1963): 216–18.

Montrose, Louis. "The Purpose of Playing: Reflections on a Shakespearean Anthropology." *Helios* n.s. 7 (1980): 51–74.

Muir, Kenneth. "A Reconstruction of *Edward III*." *Shakespeare Survey* 6 (1953): 39–47.

Mullaney, Steven. "Brothers and Others, or the Art of Alienation." In *Cannibals, Witches, and Divorce: Estranging the Renaissance*, edited by Marjorie Garber. Baltimore: Johns Hopkins University Press, 1987.

———. *The Place of the Stage: License, Play, and Power in Renaissance England*. Chicago: University of Chicago Press, 1988.

———. "Strange Things, Gross Terms, Curious Customs: The Rehearsal of Cultures in the Late Renaissance." In *Representing the English Renaissance*, edited by Stephen Greenblatt. Berkeley: University of California Press, 1988.

O'Connor, Frank. *The Road to Stratford*. London: Methuen, 1948.

Ornstein, Robert. *A Kingdom for a Stage*. Cambridge: Harvard University Press, 1972.

Outhwaite, R. B. *Inflation in Tudor and Early Stuart England*. London: Macmillan, 1969.

Palliser, David Michael. *The Age of Elizabeth: England Under the Later Tudors 1547–1603*. London: Longman, 1983.

Palmer, Barbara D. "'Ciphers to This Great Accompt': Civic Pageantry in the Second Tetralogy." In *Pageantry in the Shakespearean Theater*, edited by David M. Bergeron. Athens: University of Georgia Press, 1985.

Patterson, Annabel. *Censorship and Interpretation: The Conditions of Reading and Writing in Early Modern England*. Madison: University of Wisconsin Press, 1984.

Pierce, Robert B. *Shakespeare's History Plays: The Family and the State*. Columbus: Ohio State University Press, 1971.

Pitcher, Seymour. *The Case for Shakespeare's Authorship of "The Famous Victories of Henry V."* Albany: State University of New York Press, 1961.

Pratt, Samuel M. "Shakespeare and Humphrey Duke of Gloucester: A Study of Myth." *Shakespeare Quarterly* 16 (1965): 201–16.

Price, Jonathan R. "*King John* and Problematic Art." *Shakespeare Quarterly* 21 (1970): 25–28.

Prior, Moody E. *The Drama of Power*. Evanston, Ill.: Northwestern University Press, 1973.

Proudfoot, Richard. "Edmund Ironside." *Times Literary Supplement*, 22 October 1982, 1162.

Rabkin, Norman. "Rabbits, Ducks, and *Henry V*." *Shakespeare Quarterly* 28 (1977): 279–96.

Rackin, Phyliss. "Anti-Historians: Women's Roles in Shakespeare's Histories." *Theater Journal* 37 (1985): 329–44.

———. "The Role of the Audience in Shakespeare's *Richard II*." *Shakespeare Quarterly* 36 (1985): 262–81.

Reed, Robert R. *Crime and God's Judgment in Shakespeare.* Lexington: University Press of Kentucky, 1984.

Reese, Max Meredith. *The Cease of Majesty.* New York: St. Martin's Press, 1961.

Ribner, Irving. "Bolingbroke, A True Machiavellian." *Modern Language Quarterly* 9 (1948): 177–84.

———. *The English History Play in the Age of Shakespeare.* Princeton: Princeton University Press, 1957.

———. "The Political Problems in Shakespeare's Lancastrian Tetralogy." *Studies in Philology* 49 (1952): 171–84.

Richmond, Hugh M. *Shakespeare's Political Plays.* New York: Random House, 1967.

Ricks, Don M. *Shakespeare's Emergent Form: A Study of the Structures of the "Henry VI" Plays.* Logan: Utah State University Press, 1968.

Riggs, David. *Shakespeare's Heroical Histories: "Henry VI" and Its Literary Tradition.* Cambridge: Harvard University Press, 1971.

Rossiter, Arthur Percival. *Angel With Horns and Other Essays.* Edited by Graham Storey. New York: Theatre Arts Books, 1961.

Saccio, Peter. *Shakespeare's English Kings.* Oxford: Oxford University Press, 1977.

Sams, Eric. *Shakespeare's Lost Play, "Edmund Ironside."* New York: St. Martin's Press, 1985.

Sanders, Norman. "The True Prince and the False Thief: Prince Hal and the Shift of Identity." *Shakespeare Survey* 30 (1977): 29–34.

Scarisbrick, J. J. *The Reformation and the English People.* Oxford: Blackwell, 1984.

Schelling, Felix E. *Elizabethan Drama.* 2 vols. Boston: Houghton Mifflin, 1908.

———. *Elizabethan Playwrights.* New York: Harper, 1925.

———. *The English Chronicle Play.* 1902: New York: Haskell House, 1964.

Schlegal, August Wilhelm von. *Vorlesungen über Dramaturgische Künst und Litteratur.* 2 vols. Leipzig: Weidmann, 1846.

———. *Lectures on Dramatic Art and Literature.* Translated by John Black. 2d ed., rev. London: G. Bell, 1889.

Schucter, J. D. "Prince Hal and Francis: The Imitation of an Action." *Shakespeare Studies* 3 (1967): 129–37.

Sen Gupta, S. C. *Shakespeare's Historical Plays.* London: Oxford University Press, 1964.

Sewall, Arthur. *Character and Society in Shakespeare.* Oxford: Oxford University Press, 1951.

Shakespeare, William. *The Riverside Shakespeare.* Edited by G. Blakemore Evans. Boston: Houghton Mifflin, 1974.

Shanker, Sidney. *Shakespeare and the Uses of Ideology.* The Hague: Mouton, 1975.

Sharpe, Robert B. *The Real War of the Theaters.* Boston: Heath, 1935.

Shepherd, Simon. *Marlowe and the Politics of Elizabethan Theatre*. New York: St. Martin's Press, 1986.

Siegel, Paul N. "Falstaff and His Social Milieu." *Shakespeare Jahrbuch* 110 (1974): 139–45.

———. "Monarchy, Aristocracy and Bourgeoisie in Shakespeare History Plays." *Science and Society* 42 (1978–79): 478–82.

———. *Shakespeare's English and Roman History Plays*. Rutherford, N.J.: Fairleigh Dickinson University Press, 1986.

Simon, Joan. *Education and Society in Tudor England*. Cambridge: Cambridge University Press, 1966.

Simmons, J. L. "Shakespeare's *King John* and Its Source: Coherence, Pattern, and Vision." *Tulane Studies in English* 17 (1969): 53–72.

Smith, Robert Metcalf. *Froissart and the English Chronicle Play*. New York: Columbia University Press, 1915.

Spivack, Bernard. *Shakespeare and the Allegory of Evil*. New York: Columbia University Press, 1958.

Squibb, George Drewry. *The High Court of Chivalry*. Oxford: Oxford University Press, Clarendon Press, 1959.

Stirling, Brents. "Bolingbroke's Decision." *Shakespeare Quarterly* 2 (1951): 27–34.

———. *The Populace in Shakespeare*. New York: Columbia University Press, 1949.

Stone, Lawrence. *The Causes of the English Revolution 1529–1642*. New York: Harper and Row, 1972.

———. *The Crisis of the Aristocracy 1558–1641*. Oxford: Oxford University Press, Clarendon Press, 1965.

———. "The Educational Revolution in England, 1560–1640." *Past and Present* 28 (1964): 41–80.

———. *The Family, Sex and Marriage in England, 1500–1800*. New York: Harper and Row, 1977.

Stroud, Ronald. "The Bastard to the Time in *King John*." *Comparative Drama* 6 (1972): 154–66.

Stubblefield, Charles. "Some Thoughts About *King John*." *College English Association Critic* 35, no. 3 (1973): 25–28.

Swinburne, Algernon Charles. *A Study of Shakespeare*. London: Worthington, 1880.

Sykes, H. Dugdale. *The Authorship of "The Taming of a Shrew," "The Famous Victories of Henry V," and the Additions to Marlowe's "Faustus."* Shakespeare Association Paper, 28 February 1919. London: De La More Press, 1919.

Symonds, John Addington. *Shakespeare's Predecessors in the English Drama*. London: Smith, Elder, 1884.

Talbert, Ernest W. *Elizabethan Drama and Shakespeare's Early Plays*. Chapel Hill: University of North Carolina Press, 1963.

———. *The Problem of Order*. Chapel Hill: University of North Carolina Press, 1962.

Taylor, Gary. *To Analyze Delight*. Newark: University of Delaware Press, 1985.

Tennenhouse, Leonard. *Power on Display: The Politics of Shakespeare's Genres*. London: Methuen, 1986.

————. "Strategies of State and Political Plays: *A Midsummer Night's Dream, Henry V, Henry VIII*." In *Political Shakespeare,* edited by Jonathan Dollimore and Alan Sinfield. Ithaca: Cornell University Press, 1985.

Tillyard, Eustace M. W. *Shakespeare's History Plays.* New York: Macmillan, 1944.

Toulmin, Stephen, and June Goodfield. *The Discovery of Time.* New York: Harper and Row, 1965.

Trace, Jacqueline. "Shakespeare's Bastard Faulconbridge: An Early Tudor Hero." *Shakespeare Studies* 13 (1980): 59–69.

Traversi, Derek. *Shakespeare: From "Richard II" to "Henry V."* Stanford, Calif. Stanford University Press, 1957.

The Troublesome Reign of King John. In *Narrative and Dramatic Sources of Shakespeare,* edited by Geoffrey Bullough. Vol. 4. London: Routledge and Kegan Paul, 1962.

Turner, Robert Y. *Shakespeare's Apprenticeship.* Chicago: University of Chicago Press, 1974.

Utterback, Raymond. "Public Men, Private Wills and Kingship in *Henry VI, Part III.*" *Renaissance Papers* (1978): 47–54.

Ure, Peter, ed. *Richard II.* The Arden Shakespeare. London: Methuen, 1965.

Van de Water, Julia. "The Bastard in *King John.*" *Shakespeare Quarterly* 11 (1960): 137–46.

Vaughan, Virginia Mason. "Between Tetralogies: *King John* as Transition." *Shakespeare Quarterly* 35 (1984): 407–20.

Waith, Eugene. "*King John* and the Drama of History." *Shakespeare Quarterly* 29 (1978): 192–211.

Walch, Gunter. "*Henry V* as Working-House of Ideology." *Shakespeare Survey* 40 (1988): 63–68.

Walter, J. H., ed. *King Henry V.* The Arden Shakespeare. London: Methuen, 1954.

Ward, Adolphus William. *A History of English Dramatic Literature to the Death of Queen Anne.* 2 vols. London: Macmillan, 1875.

Ward, Adolphus William, and A. R. Waller. *The Cambridge History of English Literature.* 15 vols. Cambridge: Cambridge University Press, 1933.

Ward, Bernard M. "*The Famous Victories of Henry V:* Its Place in Elizabethan Dramatic Literature." *Review of English Literature* 4 (1928): 270–94.

Warren, Roger. "'Contrarieties Agree': An Aspect of Dramatic Technique in *Henry VI.*" *Shakespeare Survey* 37 (1984): 75–83.

Webster, Margaret. *Shakespeare Without Tears.* New York: McGraw-Hill, 1942.

Weimann, Robert. "Bifold Authority in Shakespeare's Theatre." *Shakespeare Quarterly* 39 (1988): 401–17.

————. "Discourse, Ideology and the Crisis of Authority in Post-Reformation England." *The Yearbook of Research in English and American Literature* 5 (1987): 109–40.

————. *Shakespeare and the Popular Tradition in the Theater.* Edited by Robert Schwartz. Baltimore: Johns Hopkins University Press, 1978.

Weiss, Theodore. *The Breath of Clowns and Kings.* New York: Atheneum, 1971.

Wells, Robin. *Shakespeare, Politics and the State.* London: Macmillan, 1986.

Wentersdorf, Karl. "The Conspiracy of Silence in *Henry V*." *Shakespeare Quarterly* 27 (1976): 264–87.

———. "The Date of *Edward III*." *Shakespeare Quarterly* 16 (1965): 227–31.

Williams, Raymond. Afterword to *Political Shakespeare*, edited by Jonathan Dollimore and Alan Sinfield. Ithaca: Cornell University Press, 1985.

Wilson, Frank Percy. *Marlowe and the Early Shakespeare*. Oxford: Oxford University Press, Clarendon Press, 1953.

———. *Shakespearian and Other Studies*. Edited by Helen Gardner. Oxford: Oxford University Press, Clarendon Press, 1969.

Wilson, John Dover, ed. Introduction to *King John*. The New Cambridge Shakespeare. Cambridge: Cambridge University Press, 1954.

———, ed. Introduction to *King Henry IV*. The New Cambridge Shakespeare. Cambridge: Cambridge University Press, 1955.

Wilson, Richard. "'A Mingled Yarn': Shakespeare and the Cloth Workers." *Literature and History* 12 (1986): 164–80.

Wixon, Douglas. "'Calm Words Folded Up in Smoke': Propaganda and Spectator Response in *King John*." *Shakespeare Studies* 14 (1981): 111–27.

Yeats, William Butler. *Ideas of Good and Evil*. London: Bullen, 1903.

Zeevold, W. Gordon. *Foundations of Tudor Policy*. Cambridge: Harvard University Press, 1948.

Index

Acheson, Arthur, 138, 152
Acts and Monuments (Foxe), 139
Acts of the Privy Council, 10
Adams, Joseph Quincy, 135, 152
Admiral's Men, Lord, 37, 49, 59
Albion, Robert G., 133
Allen, John W., 146, 152
Alleyn, Edward, 59
All's Well That Ends Well (Shakespeare), 74
American Shakespeare Theater: production of *Henry V*, 110
Anti-Catholicism: in *Sir John Oldcastle*, 38–40; in *Thomas, Lord Cromwell*, 55–57
Anti-French sentiment: in *1 Henry VI*, 77–78; use of French as "other" in *Henry V*, 124
Anti-intellectualism in fourteenth century, 99
Aristocracy: abrogation of aristocratic privilege in *Richard II*, 104–5; decline of, 11–12; emergence of a new form, 72; struggle against monarchical absolutism, 72–73; struggle against monarchy in *Richard II*, 105–7; *Thomas, Lord Cromwell* as an attack upon aristocratic privilege, 53–55
Armstrong, Ray L., 136, 152
Armstrong, William A., 136, 152
Arthos, John, 142, 152
Ascham, Roger, 143
Audience (Elizabethan): nature of, 9, 10, 11, 101, 122; multivalent nature of in *Henry V*, 110–11, 122, 128, 130–31; source of civil disobedience, 10, 11; variety of responses in *King John*, 88
Authorship: *Edmund Ironside*, 59–60, 69–70; *Edward III*, 28; *The Famous Victories of Henry V*, 17; *Sir John Oldcastle*, 37; *Thomas, Lord Cromwell*, 49

Baker, Herschel, 143, 152
Bell, John, 141
Barbican Theatre: production of *Romeo and Juliet*, 111
Barons' Wars, 104
Baugh, A. C., 134
Bell, Mary, 28, 136, 152
Bellamy, J. G., 147, 152
Bentley, Gerald Eades, 139, 152
Berger, Harry, 147, 152
Bergeron, David, 147, 149, 154, 159
Berman, Ronald, 142, 144, 152
Berry, Edward I., 143, 152
Bevington, David, 112, 136, 138, 140, 142, 148, 152
Billings, Wayne L., 142, 152
Bilton, Peter, 142, 143, 152
Black, John, 132, 160
Blanpied, John W., 94, 142, 144, 145, 153
Boas, Frederick S., 60, 70, 138, 139, 140, 153
Boklund, Gunner, 145, 153
Bonjour, Adrien, 93, 144, 153
Bonnard, Georges A., 146, 153
Booth, Stephen, 10, 132, 153
Boswell, Eleanore, 59, 60, 137, 153
Bourchier, John, Lord Berners, 136
Bowden, Peter J., 141, 153
Bradbrook, Muriel C., 135, 143, 153
Bradley, Andrew C., 150, 153
Braunmuller, A. R., 94
Brennen, Anthony S., 126, 150, 153
Briggs, Julia, 14, 133, 153
Bristol, Michael D., 118, 133, 149, 153
British Library, 59

165